W9-DJM-792

SLAVE LIFE IN AMERICA

A Historiography and Selected Bibliography

James S. Olson

UNIVERSITY
PRESS OF
AMERICA

LANHAM • NEW YORK • LONDON

Copyright © 1983 by

University Press of America,™ Inc.

4720 Boston Way
Lanham, MD 20706

3 Henrietta Street
London WC2E 8LU England

Library of Congress Cataloging in Publication Data

Olson, James Stuart, 1946-
  Slave life in America.

  1. Slavery—United States—Condition of slaves—
Historiography. 2. Slavery—United States—Condition
of slaves—Bibliography. 3. Slaves—United States—
Historiography. 4. Slaves—United States—Bibliography.
I. Title.
E443.044   1983   973'.0496'0072   83-4876
ISBN 0-8191-3285-3
ISBN 0-8191-3286-1 (pbk.)

To Heather

Contents

Preface   vii

1. Slavery in the United States   1

2. Slaves, Psyches, and Historians   23

3. Some Primary Sources   47

4. The Background of Slavery   61

5. The Institutions of Slavery   77

6. The World of the Slaves   99

Preface

Today, more than three centuries since the first Africans settled in the United States, the place of black people in America remains an unanswered and controversial question. None of the whites standing on the wharf at Jamestown in 1619 when those Africans disembarked realized the social and political implications of what was taking place. Ever since then, the question of race in general and black people in particular has been the central philosophical issue of American history, repeatedly confronting our social prejudices with our moral values.

At almost every turn in United States history, racial questions have affected public policy. Resentful about their legal and economic status, black people have demanded equality and justice, sometimes more vehemently than others. White people, confused and frightened, have responded reluctantly to those demands, never really certain of what role blacks would play in society, but yielding, in each generation, more and more ground in the drive for equality. Much of American history has tried to deal with that confrontation. From the time the first Quaker abolitionists condemned slavery in the eighteenth century, public controversies over race refused to disappear. The American Revolution, slavery, abolitionism, westward expansion, the Civil War, Reconstruction, the labor movement, industrialization and urbanization, imperialism, progressivism, populism, World Wars I and II, the Great Depression, poverty, and the recent civil rights movement have all grown out of or become directly involved with the larger problem of race relations. In every generation, Americans have had to deal with the issues raised by the decision to bring in the first African slaves. No doubt, the next few centuries of United States history will continue to deal with the place of black people in the larger society.

Given the significance of slavery in American history, it is not surprising that the literature is enormous. The need to analyze and explain slavery has been one of the most compelling drives in the history of American scholarship. Until the post-World War II period, public and scholarly interest in slavery was concentrated for

vii

the most part on the impact the "peculiar institution" had on white society--whether or not it caused the Civil War, whether or not it was profitable, whether or not it destined the South to permanent second-class status, whether or not it destroyed the two-party system before 1860, or whether or not it was the cause or effect of white racism. In the last few decades, the focus of much scholarly research has changed; while the older issues continue to attract interest, there is much more concern about the nature of black life under slavery. In this brief volume, I have tried to provide a comprehensive, but certainly not exhaustive, bibliography on slave life in the United States.

By focusing on the life of the slaves--their living standards, religion, families, and cultural values--I have purposely ignored the traditional topics which revolved around the white community. Consequently, there is no discussion of the politics of slavery, the abolition movement, white racial attitudes, the profitability of slavery, or the impact of slavery on southern whites. Except for the listings under "Primary Sources" in Chapter Three, I have also confined myself to secondary sources within the historical discipline. Where the research of anthropologists or sociologists has had a direct impact on the historiography of slavery, as in the writings of people like Melville Herskovits, E. Franklin Frazier, or Gunnar Myrdal, I have included them in the bibliography. Otherwise, these bibliographies consist of the research of trained historians. Finally, when an author has written a number of articles which later became part of a book, I have listed only the more inclusive publication.

James S. Olson
Huntsville, Texas

Chapter 1
Slavery in the United States

The ancestral homeland of Afro-Americans is the rain forest of West Africa and the grasslands of the northern Sudan. In 1500, West Africa was a complex mix of dozens of distinct cultures, ranging from the literate, Islamic kingdoms of the Sudan to the nonliterate, agrarian societies of the coastal rain forest. Most Africans brought to the United States as slaves were members of the agricultural tribes of West Africa: the Ibos, Ewes, Wolofs, Biafadas, Bambaras, Ibibios, Aradas, and Serers. They came from the more centralized nations of Yoruba, Hausa, Ashanti, Dahomey, Mandingo, and Fulani, as well as from the Kingdom of Songhay in the Sudan.

Most American historians for years ignored the African background of slavery, and a prevailing body of misinformation about African civilization helped whites sublimate their guilt and convince themselves that slavery was justifiable. If West African culture really had been savage and barbaric, then the slaves might actually have profited from their bondage. The stereotype of African barbarianism permitted many whites to look upon slavery as a civilizing force, a precursor of what imperialists would later describe as "the white man's burden." By removing black people from such a crude and unproductive environment, and introducing them to the refinements of European culture, white slave traders and slaveowners could reassure troubled consciences about the gross inhumanity of bondage. Indeed, some of the more callous southerners even demanded credit for assisting in the development of the world black community. Though twisted, their logic proved quite virulent, retaining even today a measure of credibility in certain circles, whether in the barber shops of the South or in the academic arguments of people like William Shockley or Arthur Jensen.

But the stereotype was just that, a racist and completely inaccurate portrait of West Africa. Indeed, the northern Sudan was a highly sophisticated society. By 1500 the Kingdom of Songhay, under the leadership of Askia Mohammed I, had become a major power, controlling West Africa south of the Sahara, from the Atlantic coast

1

in the west, through the Niger and Benue river basins, to Lake Chad in the east. Songhay was a literate, Islamic society blessed with a centralized bureaucracy, an efficient banking system, and public education from kindergarten through the University of Sankore at Timbuktu. Farmers raised sheep, cattle, okra, sorghum, and cotton; artisans manufactured jewelry, tools, textiles, pottery, and bronze castings; miners produced gold, iron ore, and copper; and merchants exported goods across the trans-Saharan trade routes to Europe. Songhay was widely recognized as an intellectual, economic, and political center in the sixteenth century.

Some slaves came from Songhay, but most Afro American slaves had their roots in the smaller states of the rain forest. Yoruba, Ashanti, Dahomey, Mossi, and Hausa enjoyed a rich variety of cultural styles and had developed far beyond any primitive nomadism. For the most part, they were very decentralized societies, with political power resting on family networks highly respectful of local prerogatives. Kings were dominant but not usually absolutist. They delegated authority to ministerial assistants drawn from the noble families. Only rarely, as in Dahomey, did a king establish absolute power. Social structures were similarly decentralized, with life revolving around extended families. Kinship loyalties were strong and most people projected them into the next world, making ancestor worship an integral part of religion. Finally, their economies were stable and productive. On coastal farms people raised yams, carrots, and potatoes; near the Sudanese grasslands they produced wheat and cotton. Others raised sheep and cattle, fished, and manufactured rugs, cloth, pottery, and iron tools. They were self-sufficient, labor specialized, and their standard of living well above that of primitive, nomadic societies. When Europeans moved into West Africa, they encountered highly developed societies whose political, social, and economic institutions were functioning well.

The Europeans came, of course, in a desperate search for slave labor. In the Americas, slavery was both an economic and social institution; its origins were deeply rooted in the American environment and in the social and religious values of the European colonists. Unlike Europe, where labor was abundant and land precious, America had just the opposite: an abundance of land and a shortage of labor. For most white men, the acquisition of land was relatively easy. The South, with its fertile soil and long growing season, was especially suited for large-scale commercial agriculture. And with European

2

demand for tobacco, rice, indigo, and cotton apparently insatiable, commercial plantations prevailed there soon after colonization. But this was also a pre-industrial society, highly dependent upon labor rather than technology. In America, the labor was unavailable, primarily because wage levels for agricultural workers were too high and because most colonists preferred to acquire land of their own. If southern farmers were to prosper, they needed workers who would not demand high wages, or be inclined to leave the plantation, or aspire to higher callings. Free laborers would hardly meet these requirements, and slavery seemed the only solution.

But who would serve as slaves? During the colonial period, plantation owners used white indentured servants but they usually proved unsatisfactory. They were initially expensive, often escaped to nearby cities, and eventually worked out their contracts in a few years and were free to go. The concept of lifetime servitude for white workers also offended the racial sensibilities of some plantation owners reluctant to exploit "their own kind." What they needed was a racial minority, one easily recognizeable in the society and one which would not generate feelings of guilt among slaveowners.

Native Americans seemed to fill those requirements. Their physical characteristics certainly distinguished them from the larger white society, and very few whites had any qualms about exploiting them. But there were problems with Indian slavery. There were simply not enough of them. Only 700,000 Indians were left by 1700, and not all of them were accustomed to a sedentary agricultural life. Even among tribes familiar with farming, cultural values often predisposed men against the idea of agricultural labor. With their lack of immunity to European diseases, many Indians could not survive contact with whites; epidemic deaths devastated tribal society. Finally, the Indians knew the land and could escape with relative ease. Instead, plantation owners in the South began looking for a people who were racially distinct, conditioned to commercial agriculture, not familiar with the American environment, and immune to European diseases. It did not take them long to look toward Africa as the source of their slaves.

English racism and ethnocentrism made the whole process of slavery a morally acceptable activity. The relationship between slavery and prejudice is a complex one, with scholars still arguing whether slavery created prejudice or simply reinforced existing beliefs about racial inferiority. But from their very first contacts

with Africans in the sixteenth century, the English responded negatively, with surprise and then suspicion.
Long before plantations had created a demand for slaves,
the English were prejudiced toward black people.

The evolution of that prejudice was slow, and color
was an important ingredient. For centuries Western culture has instinctively attached meaning to various col-
ors, usually to describe emotional moods and moral values. Red, for example, suggests anger or sensuality,
and green has symbolized envy. But the most powerful
associations are those connected with black and white.
Black has usually been linked with fear, evil, sin, and
death, and white with purity, chastity, light, and truth.
People still think of white as good and black as bad. A
1972 edition of Webster's New World Dictionary defines
"black" as "totally without light; soiled; dirty; evil;
wicked; harmful; disgraceful; sad; dismal; gloomy; without hope." Psychologists hardly agree about the emotional dynamics of color association. Some believe the
aversion to blackness is tied to childhood fears of the
dark--of loneliness and abandonment--while neo-Freudians
argue that white people associate blackness with defe-
cating, a repulsive act in Western society. Whatever
the reasons, skin color became a critical element in
racism, and English literature well back into the Middle
Ages reflected that bias. The dark skin color of the
Africans psychologically stimulated some of those fears
in the English mind.

But there was more to the racism than color association. Most Europeans, and especially the English because of their geographic isolation from the Continent,
were intensely ethnocentric, attaching moral significance to cultural differences and making their own values
the frame of reference for measuring virtue. They examined African culture--homes, food, clothes, language,
and sexual practices--and found them "savage" and "primitive," certainly unworthy of acceptance as peers and
equals. Few of the English had any doubts that the
African way of life was inferior. They also disapproved
of African religions. Sixteenth-century Protestantism
left little room for toleration. To the English, the
Africans were "heathens," misguided children destined
for hell because of their "bizarre" and even "satanic"
religious loyalties. With its magic and mysticism, its
worship of idols, ancestors, and the elements, African
religion seemed sacrilegious and "anti-Christ." Joined
with the negative impressions left by African skin color,
the images of African "savagery" and "heathenism" generated a powerful racism in the English mind.

So while the American environment created a demand
for involuntary servants, English racism turned American eyes to Africa as the source of the slaves. That
the Africans were numerous, accustomed to settled agriculture and quite adept at it, and relatively immune to
European diseases made them even more likely candidates
for slavery. The racism was so virulent and the convic-
tions of African moral depravity so certain among the
English that it was relatively easy for them to convince
themselves that slavery would be a boon to the slaves--
a way for them to escape their blighted background and
be introduced to a more civilized society.

Although the Portuguese, to supply their Brazilian
sugar plantations, began the trans-Atlantic slave trade,
and the Dutch often served as middlemen, it was the English who came to dominate the traffic. Late in the seventeenth century, after tobacco plantations were thriving in Maryland and Virginia and sugar plantations in
the West Indies, England chartered the Royal African
Company to break the Portuguese and Dutch monopolies on
the slave trade. With enormous economic resources and
the protection of the English navy, the Royal African
Company did just that. Until its demise in the nineteenth century, the Atlantic slave trade was dominated
by the British.

There were several stages in the Atlantic slave
trade. First, the slaves had to be captured, and for
the most part the English traders left that task up to
other Africans. Tribal rivalries in West Africa were intense and bitter, and human bondage was nothing new to
the region. For centuries West Africans had owned and
traded slaves. The major difference, however, between
West African and American slavery involved capitalism
and racism. Most slaves in West Africa were house servants captured in war; the local economy did not depend
on a continuous flow of slave laborers for survival.
Also, despite tribal rivalries, West Africans at least
shared skin color. Opportunities for adoption, freedom,
and marital assimilation were relatively good. Rigid,
permanent caste systems based on race and massive labor
exploitation did not develop in West Africa as they did
in the New World. Slavery was not the harsh, exploitive
institution it became in the Americas. At first, the
slave trade was even a casual affair; Africans simply
sold their prisoners of war to the English. By the
eighteenth century, however, the trading had assumed
economic importance and had become a major cause of war
in West Africa as coastal tribes competed to supply the
New World plantations.

5

The second stage of the slave trade involved moving the captives from the African interior to the coastal exchange posts. This too was handled largely by West Africans since few whites were interested in venturing deep into the countryside. Their lives were worth very little there. Along the way to the coast, the slaves changed hands several times as African middlemen exacted their own profits. When they reached the coast, the English bought them with rum, cotton cloth, guns, gunpowder, cowrie shells, brass rings, and pig iron. Slavery had become big business for Africans as well as for Europeans.

After plying the African coast for several months acquiring their human cargo, the slave ships would turn west and head for the Americas. This was the third stage, known infamously now as the "Middle Passage." Hundreds of slaves were crowded into the dark, damp hold of the slave ship for months at a time, with little exercise, subsistence diets, and absolutely no sanitary facilities. The death rate from flu, dysentary, smallpox, pleurisy, and pneumonia was devastating. Thousands died from "fixed melancholy," a form of mental depression in which victims simply lost the will to survive. Twenty percent of the Africans did not survive the Middle Passage, and officials within the Royal African Company often debated the merits of "loose pack" as opposed to "tight pack." In "tight pack," slaves were crowded densely into the ship's hold, and although the mortality rate would be quite high, the initial numbers were substantial enough to guarantee a profitable supply of surviving slaves at voyage's end. Advocates of the "loose pack" were convinced that by crowding fewer slaves into the hold, mortality rates would be reduced and the return on initial investment maximized. Since perhaps ten million slaves were taken from Africa to all the colonies in the New World between 1600 and 1800, it can be assumed that two million died in transit. It definitely was, as one European trader recalled, "a dreadful business."

The final stage in the movement of people from Africa to the United States was the "seasoning" process in the West Indies. Most African slaves brought into the United States had spent a period of from several months to several years working the sugar plantations of the West Indies before their arrival in America. There, through a variety of techniques, Africans were "taught" the rhythm and nature of slave life, how to work long hours in regimented gangs, how to acquiesce to white power, how to speak English, and how to "accept" their lot in

life. The mortality rate among newly arrived slaves in
the West Indies ran as high as thirty percent. After
the "breaking in" process in the Caribbean, they were
then transported to and sold in the United States.

Dutch merchants delivered the first Africans to Virginia in 1619, but because of certain economic and social circumstances, they were treated as indentured servants and not as slaves. Instead of lifetime servitude,
they were released after seven to ten years of work.
Gradually, however, throughout the seventeenth century,
as the plantation economy emerged in Virginia and Maryland, the demand for cheap labor intensified. The time
of service for black servants slowly increased, dis-
tinguishing them from white indentured servants. At the
same time, as the heightened demand for cheap labor
brought more and more Africans into the southern colonies, the level of white fears about the black population
intensified. The need to control the black population,
to guarantee the safety of the white community from the
strange, black Africans, soon became as important a dimension of slavery as the economic one. Between 1619
and 1660, laws prohibiting interracial sex and the pos-
session of firearms by black people began to appear in
Virginia. Other laws restricted black access to alcohol,
imposed curfews on them, and outlawed public gatherings.
In 1661 the Virginia House of Burgesses called for lifetime servitude in certain cases and shortly thereafter
declared that the children of lifetime servants inherited
their parents' legal status. At first lifetime slavery
was reserved for rebellious or criminal blacks, but by
1700 it had become common throughout the country and
meant hereditary servitude as well. Slave codes became
more and more severe during the 1700s. Soon the law
viewed slaves as property, people without civil liberties
and subject to the legal control of their masters.

As tobacco, rice, and indigo plantations developed,
black indentured service seemed increasingly uneconomi-
cal. By requiring service for life, the planters eliminated labor turnover and protected their investment.
Formal slavery also gave whites the sense of control
they needed over blacks. In the northern colonies,
where black people numbered less than five percent of
the population in 1750, there was little insecurity;
but it was different in the South. Black people were
only two percent of the Virginia population in 1640, but
thirty-one percent in 1715, and over forty percent in
1770. It was similar in Maryland, the Carolinas, and
Georgia. Whites were caught in an ironic trap. They
feared the growth of the black population but believed

7

it was economically necessary. Black indentured servitude was expensive and potentially dangerous because the Africans would have children and would someday be free, out of the legal control of their planter-owners. Whites worried constantly about the prospects of having thousands of free blacks living beyond the authority of the plantations. If all blacks were slaves, however, they would be under white control and supposedly less threatening to the white community. Not surprisingly, during the last half of the seventeenth century, whites transformed black indentured servitude into lifetime, hereditary slavery.

The economic, political, and religious structure of life in the United States made that control more influential and absolute than in many other parts of the New World. Unlike European societies and most of the colonies in the Americas, the British North American colonies placed a great premium on capitalism, federalism, and Protestantism, all of which were devoted to decentralized systems of authority. Free enterprise capitalism worshipped private property, the right of an individual to use and dispose of his personal property according exclusively to personal whim. As for political authority, the American colonies and later the states believed in federalism--the right of local political units to control their own police powers. Finally, the essence of Protestantism was congregational sovereignty, the right of local religious communities rather than centralized religious bureaucracies to make decisions affecting the group. The effect of these economic, political, and religious systems was to localize authority, to prevent distant, centralized groups from intervening in people's lives. As for the institution of slavery in the United States, there turned out to be no monarchy, nobility, church, or corporate elite capable of regulating or ameliorating it. Slaves were largely under the absolute control of the local planter class in the southern colonies.

Deterioration in the treatment of slaves was especially serious in the South. Slavery was comparatively mild in New England, where slaves could join the Congregational Church, have their marriages legally recognized, and receive limited educations. To a lesser extent, New Jersey, Delaware, and Pennsylvania treated slaves with some measure of liberality. That was not so in New York City because blacks made up nearly fifteen percent of the population. Racial tensions there were serious and the corresponding slave codes rather severe. The black people of New York City were carefully controlled. But for the Middle Colonies, with only ten percent of the population black and the Quakers demanding humane treatment, race relations were much better than in the South.

These changes in the legal and social status of black people came at a time when Africans were assuming increasingly important roles in southern life. In the earliest stages of the colonial era, blacks and whites had often worked closely together just to survive. Since the climate and flora of West Africa generally resembled those of the South, blacks were able to make important contributions to colonial life. West Africans helped introduce rice cultivation to South Carolina, and Guinea corn was mixed with native Indian varieties. Blacks were highly trusted in the area of animal husbandry because of their West African backgrounds. Very familiar with swamps and marshes, the Africans showed Europeans how to poison rivers and streams temporarily with quicklime in order to catch fish. Like they had done back home, the Africans used alligators to protect livestock. Blacks also introduced the use of herbs and some natural medicines to the colonies, engaged actively in the fur trade as Indians disappeared, and served in most colonial militias during the seventeenth century.

While providing whites with some economic security, slavery at the same time made them nervous and troubled their consciences. But in an extraordinary paradox, slavery permitted white planters to join in the rhetoric of democracy. Because Africans were occupying the very bottom of the social ladder, rigidly isolated into a fixed caste, whites were able to support full civil liberties for all other whites, regardless of their economic circumstances. Exploitation of slaves was so easy that the planter class could at least pay lip service to white democracy. Human bondage was ironically promoting the democratic ideology. Throughout the history of the South, wealthy white landowners would play on the racial fears of poor whites. Whenever poor whites even considered an economic or political struggle for power with wealthy whites, the rich whites would bring up the issue of race, always holding out to poor whites their "elite" social and political status even though they were suffering from poverty. Slavery was permitting a plutocratic society to sustain a democratic value system, even though those values did not often translate into equality for poor whites.

The American Revolution then undermined even that assumption. By 1776 the colonists were maturing politically. From England they had acquired ideas of representative government, the evil nature of political power, and the unalienable rights of man, and when England violated those rights after 1763, the colonists became revolutionaries willing to resort to violence. But the egalitarian philosophy came into direct conflict with the institution of slavery. Throughout much of the eighteenth century Philadelphia Quakers had condemned slavery. At the same time, the Enlightenment emphasis on reason and natural rights made the legal justifications for slavery seem increasingly hollow. Finally, evangelical Protestantism in the North inspired a spirit of abolition by advocating charity toward all people. During the American Revolution, these forces gained credibility because of the inconsistency of denouncing oppression while condoning human bondage. How could Americans criticize English oppression when 500,000 blacks were slaves? The hypocrisy was all too evident, and after 1776 people like Thomas Paine, Benjamin Franklin, Thomas Jefferson, James Otis, John Adams, Noah Webster, and John Jay all denounced slavery.

The military service of thousands of blacks during the Revolution also touched the conscience of America. Crispus Attucks, a runaway slave, was shot and killed at the Boston Massacre in 1770 and became the first American to die at the hands of British soldiers. Peter Salem and Salem Poore, both slaves freed to fight in the Continental Army, distinguished themselves for valor at Bunker Hill, as did Lemuel Haynes at the Battle of Ticonderoga and "Pompey" at the Battle of Stony Point. Manpower shortages forced state after state to free slaves who would volunteer to fight. Eventually more than five thousand blacks fought with colonial forces, participating in every engagement from Lexington in 1775 to Yorktown in 1781. Their faithful service on behalf of the colonies even more clearly exposed the hypocrisy of human bondage in a democratic society.

The ideological momentum generated by the American Revolution then joined with economic and social forces to destroy slavery in the North. After the Revolution, northern agriculture and industry gradually became capital rather than labor intensive, relying on machines instead of people whenever possible. Because wheat, corn, livestock, and other grain farms as well as most of the eastern factories did not depend exclusively on slave labor, the economic foundation of slavery died. White people in the North could give up their slaves, especially their house servants, without suffering irreparable economic loss. Conveniently, their revolutionary ideology did not encounter any economic obstacles.

Nor was there any compelling social rationale to continue slavery. The black population of the North was too small to threaten white society, so northern whites did not have the compulsion to control black society. There were only 75,000 blacks out of nearly 1,500,000 people in the North in 1776, and the ratio declined to only 250,000 blacks out of 20,000,000 northerners in 1860. Not often frightened by the black minority, whites did not resist abolition as intensely as southerners did. Vested social and economic interests had rather little to lose from freeing the slaves.

For all these reasons a powerful movement arose in the North. Quakers organized the first antislavery society in 1775, and in 1780 Pennsylvania provided for the gradual abolition of slavery. Massachusetts abolished slavery by court order in 1783, and the next year Connecticut and Rhode Island passed general abolition laws. New York and New Jersey enacted similar laws in 1785 and 1786, and in 1787 the Northwest Ordinance prohibited slavery in the Ohio Valley. After fierce debate in 1787, the Constitutional Convention outlawed the importation of slaves after 1807. The American Revolution brought freedom from England and, for northern blacks, freedom from bondage.

Legal freedom, however, did not mean equality. In Ohio, Indiana, and Illinois white settlers from the South segregated free blacks whenever possible. White workers there feared economic competition from blacks, and black youths were often placed in long-term apprenticeships closely resembling slavery. Black adults could not serve on juries or vote, and immigration of blacks from other states was barred. Between 1807 and 1837 New Jersey, Connecticut, New York, Rhode Island, and Pennsylvania passed laws disfranchising blacks. And throughout the North black people were segregated in public facilities and widely discriminated against in the job market. The North was hardly the promised land.

Still, slavery there was dead as a legal institution. In the South, on the other hand, the revolutionary ideology had not been strong enough to overcome the force of economic and social circumstance. Abolition was stillborn there. A small but vocal antislavery movement developed in the upper South during the Revolution, but it died out after 1800 because slavery was still justified, at least as far as the planter class was concerned, on both economic and social terms. Just as the economic need for slaves was disappearing in the North, southern dependence on cheap labor was increasing. With their soil exhausted and world markets glutted in the 1790s, tobacco farmers were looking desperately for another commercial crop. The Industrial Revolution was stimulating demand for cotton, but the South could not fill it because removing seeds from the fiber was too time-consuming and expensive. Eli Whitney solved that problem in 1793 with the cotton gin. The gin removed the seeds without destroying the cotton fiber, and cotton quickly became the South's major cash crop. Production increased from 4,000 bales in 1790 to more than five million bales in 1860. The southern plantation economy depended on having millions of black slaves in the cotton fields each day. Although thousands of white planters no doubt recognized the revolutionary ideology and the hypocrisy of slavery in a democratic society, their vision could not see beyond their pocketbooks. The ideology of freedom foundered on the rocks of profit and capital investment.

Southerners also opposed abolition for social reasons. By 1860 there were four million blacks to only seven million whites in the South. In Virginia, Texas, and Arkansas, whites outnumbered blacks by three to one, but in Mississippi and South Carolina blacks outnumbered whites. The population was divided almost equally in Louisiana, Alabama, Florida, and Georgia. The size of the black population seemed ominous; whites were obsessed with fears of slave uprisings, and only slavery gave them absolute control, or at least as much control as possible, over black people. Emancipation was out of the question.

Instead of abolition, slavery thrived in the South. Living conditions were primitive and mental pressures intense. The decisions of whites often invaded the privacy of social and family life. Black men were not permitted full decision-making power in their homes; black women had to work in the fields even when their children were young, and were sometimes exploited sexually by white men; children had to go to work at an early age; and family members could be sold separately at any time. The South outlawed any education for slaves, hoping that illiteracy would keep them dependent on their white owners. Typical food rations for field hands were four pounds of pork fat, a peck of corn meal, and a small amount of coffee and molasses each week; they usually had one dress or two shirts and one pair of trousers; and they lived in damp, small shanty homes in the "quarters." There were few rewards and few incentives.

But whites had to provide at least a subsistence

living for their property, if only to protect their investment. Planters also had a vested interest in plantation stability because it boosted productivity; very unhappy slaves or slaves who hated an overseer were inefficient workers. A few positive incentives existed, such as promises of extra rations, extra clothes, or individual garden plots, as did a number of negative encouragements: threats of whipping, incarceration, and worst of all, forced sale of family members. Slaves resisted their bondage, but for fear of losing their families, their rebellion usually took subtle forms. To avoid field work, many convinced their masters that they were naturally lazy, clumsy, and irresponsible people from whom little could be expected. Some slaves injured farm animals, broke tools, and disabled wagons to postpone work. Others even hurt themselves, inflicting wounds on their hands or legs to avoid being overworked or sold. Feigning illness was common. Thousands of slaves also ran away, hoping to reach the North or Canada on the "underground railroad"--a group of whites and free blacks who assisted runaway slaves. And there were hundreds of slave rebellions. From the 1712 uprising in New York City, which killed nine whites, to Nat Turner's rebellion in 1831, which resulted in the deaths of sixty Virginia whites, discontented slaves often used violence to try to liberate themselves. Still, such rebellions were relatively rare; slave resistance was more often directed at ameliorating the conditions of slavery than at liberation.

Despite the intense psychological pressures exerted by slavery, there was another Afro-American world, one which existed within the slave quarters, far from white society. "From sundown to sunup" a special slave culture appeared, part African and part American, which eased the trauma of bondage, provided group solidarity and status, verbalized aggression, and demonstrated love. The slaves' relationship with whites during the workday was secondary to their relationships with one another, and scholarly theories describing the slave personality only in terms of white society overlook the primary environment of the quarters. There blacks developed ethical and family values, positive self-images, and group unity. Shared customs, recreation, language, religion, and family life were the foundations of that Afro-American culture.

In terms of social customs, a number of Old World traditions had survived the Middle Passage from Africa. The practice of carrying infants by one arm with the child's legs straddling the mother's hips was an African

13

custom, and so was coiling, a technique for sewing wool-
en trays. Special styles for braiding hair came from
West Africa, as did the wearing of head kerchiefs by
black women. People from different tribes from all over
West Africa had been thrown together, and a "black" melt-
ing pot of fused customs had emerged.

An Afro-American language developed as well. Except
for isolated words (such as the West African "okay,"
which became "OK" to most Americans) or the dialects of
the most isolated Afro-American communities (such as the
Sea Islanders of Georgia and South Carolina), few African words survived in America. The slaves spoke English, but it was an English unique in pronunciation,
grammar, and morphology. Black English tended to eliminate predicate verbs, so that such statements as "He is
fat" or "He is bad" became "He fat" or "He bad." Slave
grammar neglected possessive constructions, saying "Jim
hat" rather than "Jim's hat" or "George dog" rather than
"George's dog," and it ignored gender pronouns and used
"him" and "he" for both the masculine and feminine. West
African dialects had been similar to one another in
structure, so in the United States the slaves generally
used an English vocabulary but placed it in a grammatical context which was both English and African in its
origins.

Leisure time permitted slaves to play social roles
different from that of driven servants. In the evenings
they gathered to visit and gossip, or to sing and dance;
and on Sundays and holidays they hunted, fished, gambled,
attended church, or had afternoon picnics and parties.
Most excelled in something--racing, storytelling, sing-
ing, dancing, preaching, or teaching--and enjoyed pres-
tige from such talents. Leisure activities offered a
respite from the drudgery of the fields, a liberation
from the emotional pressures of bondage.

The West African roots of slave religion and family
provided an even more meaningful structure to slave life.
In the black cultures of Guiana, Haiti, and Brazil, where
slaves vastly outnumbered and rarely saw whites, African
customs thrived; but in the United States, where whites
outnumbered blacks and racial contacts were frequent,
slaves often adopted the outer forms of European social
life but adapted its spirit to their own African and New
World experiences. Threads of African secular culture
survived in slave stories, games, dances, jokes, and folk
beliefs and provided blacks with a rich verbal literature
to express their joys and frustrations. Whites did not
try to suppress that literature because it seemed trivial

14

to them. Music, for example, was central to slave life
and accompanied daily activities--work, play, and church
services. It was functional and improvisational, symbolically related to group solidarity and individual as-
pirations. In their songs the slaves retained the form
and spirit of their African origins, fashioning expres-
sive modes for dealing with the New World. Spirituals
and secular songs helped slaves express their anger or
despair, feelings which whites would not have tolerated
in regular speech. Often whites had no idea what the
lyrics of slave songs implied, but to blacks their mean-
was quite clear.

Religion especially liberated slaves from the world
of whites and allowed them to express their deepest
feelings. Slave religion made few distinctions between
the secular and the spiritual, between this life and the
next, and symbolically carried slaves back in history to
more glorious times and forward into a more benign fu-
ture, linking them with the cosmos and assuring them that
there was justice in the universe. Except for proud,
first-generation Africans holding tenaciously to their
Old World faiths, most slaves converted to fundamental
Protestantism, while imbuing it with an emotional spirit
all their own. Since the idea of being possessed by a
spirit was common in West Africa, the revivalistic flavor of fundamental Protestantism--with its handclapping,
rhythmic body movements, public testimonies, speaking in
tongues, and conscious presence of the Holy Ghost--ap-
pealed to the slaves. They particularly were loyal to
the Baptists and Methodists because those two denomina-
tions sponsored the development of black clergies.

Some white planters encouraged religion as a tool of
social control and white ministers preached bondage as
the will of God. Patience, obedience, submissiveness,
and gratitude were the themes of white-sponsored slave
religion. But the slaves were not fooled. In white
churches they went through the motions of reverent attention, but they were rarely taken in by the thinly-
veiled messages of white preachers bent on molding them
into submission. Instead they used the white church services to visit with friends and family from other farms
or plantations, which they could rarely do at other times
because the rigid pass laws confined them to their master's property.

When permitted to worship on their own, the slaves
reinterpreted Christianity to suit their own needs.
While whites seemed preoccupied with guilt and sin, the
slaves emphasized the redeeming features of salvation;

while whites talked of eternal damnation, the slaves delighted in the story of the Jews' deliverance from bondage in Egypt. Rejecting Calvinist notions of predestination, unworthiness, sin, and damnation as well as the Paulinian doctrines of dutiful obedience and passive acceptance of social place, slave spirituals sang of redemption, glory, freedom, change, and justice. Not obsessed with guilt and depravity, black ministers spoke of the spiritual equality of all people and God's uncompromising love for everyone. Threatened on all sides by a hostile environment, the slaves united the next world with this one and bound themselves into a single community, a "chosen people" loved by God. Slave religion allowed blacks to vent the frustrations of bondage, united them in a sense of mission, and recognized them as individuals. Theirs was a spiritual world of deliverance, of Moses leading a special people to freedom and Jesus saving them from a corrupt world.

Closely related to slave religion was the world of folk tales, voodoo, magic, and spirits. African culture had always assumed that all life had direction and that apparently random events were part of a larger cosmic plan which people could understand by reading the "signs" in nature and human affairs. People were part of a natural pantheon of life. All things had causes and could be controlled by human intervention. Slaves used folk beliefs and folk medicine to heal the sick, and some folk practitioners were highly respected. Certain signs--an owl's screech, a black cat crossing one's path, the approach of a cross-eyed person--indicated bad luck ahead, which could be remedied by such devices as spitting, crossing fingers, turning pockets inside out, or turning shoes upside down on the porch. Dreams had great significance. The world of magic and voodoo gave slaves a sense of power over their masters, for in the hexes, signs, and punishments of the supernatural they tried to control the behavior of whites and their own destiny. To blacks African folk culture offered a degree of power, a means of integrating life and transcending their enslavement.

Finally, in the slave family, Afro-Americans found companionship, love, esteem, and sexual fulfillment--things the master-slave relationship denied them. Despite the breakup of families through the sale of slaves, white sexual exploitation of slave women, and incursions on the authority of black parents, the family was the basic institution of slave society. Although antebellum slave society tolerated premarital sexual liaisons, marital infidelity was strictly forbidden. Once two people

16

had "jumped the broomstick," fidelity was expected. Most slave families consisted of two parents, most slave marriages were sound--when husband and wife were allowed to stay together--and most black children traced their family line back through their fathers. If the native African family had often been polygamous and matriarchal, its American counterpart was monogamous and patriarchal. The father exercised discipline and supplemented the family diet by hunting and fishing, and the mother was responsible for household duties and raising youngsters. Although kinship systems were disrupted by the Middle Passage, blacks developed extended kinship ties in the United States. Elderly people were afforded a degree of respect unknown in white families; similarly, uncles, aunts, and cousins played more important roles in black than in white families. Under slavery the black family was the center of social life, not the debilitated institution many people have described. That former slaves eagerly had their marriages legalized after the Civil War and searched the country over to reunite separated families confirmed the loyalty of parents, children, and spouses.

Ultimately, it was the Civil War which destroyed chattel slavery in the United States. Ever since the colonial period economic interest and political philosophy had divided the North and the South into distinct regional entities. Committed to a commercial, agrarian economy and international export markets, and highly dependent on slave labor as their major capital investment, the South had never seen the need for a national bank, high protective tariffs, internal improvements, or any other measures designed to stimulate industry and technology. Most southerners were extremely loyal to a regional locale, and most southern politicians preached laissez-faire, states' rights, and a strict interpretation of the Constitution to prevent preferential treatment of northern manufacturers and federal intervention in their way of life. With a mixed economy of farming, commerce, and manufacturing, the North favored protective tariffs, a strong national bank, and federally financed internal improvements. Periodically in American history--the debate over the Articles of Confederation in the late 1770s, the Constitutional Convention in 1787, the controversy over Hamiltonian proposals in the 1790s, the Panics of 1819, 1837, and 1857, or the Jacksonian debates over the national bank and the tariff in the 1830s--the North and South had argued heatedly over the merits of their region and their economic and political points of view, but never had their differences threatened the Union.

17

But when the issue of slavery was added to these differences, civil war erupted. Slavery was the foundation of southern society, creating a static caste system different from the more open class system of the North. Slavery also contradicted the ideas of democracy, equality, and freedom. Some northerners attacked it as a moral evil, while many southerners defended it as a positive good, a way of preserving white culture and introducing black people to Christian civilization.

The national debate over slavery was at first quite cautious. People like William Lloyd Garrison and Frederick Douglass demanded the immediate abolition of slavery throughout the country, but most northerners refused to go along with such a radical disruption of southern life. Instead they chose more gradual schemes. In 1816 several northern reformers established the American Colonization Society to resettle blacks in Africa. By 1860 the society had sent several thousand blacks to Liberia. Most free blacks hated the idea on the grounds that they had the same rights as any other native-born American to live in the United States. Other northerners wanted gradual abolition and compensation to slaveholders for the loss of their slaves. The South would have nothing to do with either program, for both meant the end of slave labor in their economy.

After a while most northerners had decided that immediate abolition, gradual abolition, and colonization were naive, impractical solutions to slavery. They decided instead just to stop the expansion of slavery into the western territories, to contain slavery in the Old South where it might gradually die out on its own. The Liberty Party of 1840 and 1844, the Free Soil Party of 1848, and the Republican Party--organized in 1854--committed themselves to that objective. Southerners, on the other hand, fervently believed that for slavery and the plantation system to survive they would have to have access to fresh soil, with their slaves along, in the West.

The political struggle between the North and the South also reflected attitudes toward the composition of American society. A few northern whites opposed the expansion of slavery into the territories because they believed slavery was immoral and that any measures which strengthened it were equally evil. But they were joined by millions of others who opposed the expansion of slavery for economic reasons--free white workers afraid that slavery would eliminate jobs and undermine wage levels. Most northern whites were also racists who did not like blacks in general and opposed the expansion of slavery because it would bring blacks near their homes. Confining slavery to the South would guarantee free territories and a largely white society where the entrepreneurial instincts of Yankee culture could flourish. Southern whites, convinced that containment of slavery was a step toward abolition, and terrified by the prospects of having four million free blacks in the South, insisted on the right to carry slaves into the territories, which the Dred Scott decision by the Supreme Court in 1857 permitted them to do. Southerners were also convinced that the containment of slavery would assure the triumph of Yankee commercialism and its faith in technological change, material progress, and democratic egalitarianism, none of which they could tolerate.

Between 1820 and 1860 every sectional crisis in the United States--the Missouri Compromise of 1820, the Texas annexation, the Mexican War of 1846, the Compromise of 1850, the Kansas-Nebraska Act of 1854, and the Dred Scott decision of 1857--revolved around the question of slavery in the territories. When the Republican candidate Abraham Lincoln won the presidential election of 1860 on a platform of free soil, protective tariffs, a national banking system, and internal improvements in the form of transcontinental railroads, white southerners felt threatened socially, economically, and politically. The South panicked and seceded from the Union.

The ensuing Civil War resolved, legally at least, the status of black people in the United States. At first President Lincoln's war objectives were quite narrowly defined. He was convinced that war had broken out because southerners had insisted on carrying their slaves to the West. The North was fighting to prevent that and bring the seceded South back into the Union. Preservation of the Union, not abolition, was the central issue as far as Lincoln was concerned. Suspicious of radical social change and a racist himself who doubted the abilities of black people to rise above a servant status, Abraham Lincoln consistently opposed abolition schemes in the early months of the war. When General John C. Fremont entered Missouri in 1861 and freed the slaves, Lincoln angrily rescinded the order, and the next year he nullified General David Hunter's abolition order in Georgia, South Carolina, and Florida.

But the momentum for emancipation became irresistible after a number of pressures transformed the Civil War into a struggle to preserve the Union as well as to liberate the slaves. Most northerners, including the president, had anticipated a brief, conclusive war in which superior northern forces would overwhelm the Confederacy. But after staggering defeats at Bull Run and in the Shenandoah Valley in 1861 and 1862, a war of attrition developed. Lincoln began to see emancipation as a way of disrupting the southern economy by depriving the Confederacy of four million slaves.

Political and ideological concerns also pushed him toward emancipation. Republican abolitionists in his own party were steadily gaining strength by denouncing the hypocrisy of proclaiming democracy while condoning slavery. Radical Republicans including Thaddeus Stevens, Charles Sumner, Wendell Phillips, and Benjamin Wade insisted that Lincoln abolish slavery and were outraged when he nullified military abolition orders. Lincoln was in deep political trouble. Military defeats had dissipated his popularity, and a powerful wing of his own party was condemning his insensitivity to the plight of black people. If he was to be renominated in 1864, he had to revive his popularity and attract some Radical support. Abolition might do it. By appearing as a moral crusader rather than just a politician, Lincoln hoped to shore up his crumbling political fortunes.

But regaining Radical Republican support posed a new dilemma. Abolition would please the Radicals, but if Lincoln freed the slaves he would sacrifice the support of Democrats loyal to the Union in Delaware, Maryland, Kentucky, and Missouri--slaveowners who had opposed secession. Abolition might win renomination, but it would just as surely cost Lincoln the general election. Some way of satisfying Radical Republicans without alienating loyal slaveowning Democrats in the border states had to be developed. Lincoln slowly moved toward partial emancipation. In the spring of 1862 he supported congressional abolition of slavery in the District of Columbia and in the territories. Finally, on January 1, 1863, he issued the Emancipation Proclamation, liberating only the slaves in the rebellious states. The 400,000 slaves in loyal border states remained slaves. Lincoln thus gained Radical support without estranging border Democrats.

In April 1865 the Union armies trapped General Robert E. Lee's troops near Appomattox Court House in Virginia. The Confederacy was dead and Lee surrendered. The national nightmare was finally over. More than 600,000 young men and $15 billion had disappeared in the smoke of destruction, and the South was a pocked no-man's land of untilled farms, broken machinery, gutted buildings, fresh graves, worthless money, and defeated people. Only southern blacks were hopeful that a new age of liberty and equality was dawning. They were wrong, of course, even after ratification of the Thirteenth Amendment in December 1865 finally abolished slavery throughout the country. Slavery was dead, but equality was still a long way off in the future.

Chapter 2
Slaves, Psyches, and Historians

More than a century since the end of chattel slavery, historians remain preoccupied with the "peculiar institution," not only because of its inherent interest but because questions of race and ethnicity continue to play so central a role in American life. The discussion has been a lively one, animating classrooms, professional meetings, "smokers," and scholarly journals, occasionally even breaking into the mass media, as with the publication of Robert Fogel and Stanley Engerman's *Time on the Cross* in 1974. For every conceiveable topic, from the extent of the slave trade to the profitability of slavery, the scholarly exploration of the past has inspired intense and sometimes bitter debate. No phase of that debate has been more controversial than the impact of bondage on the personality and culture of black people in the United States. In the twentieth century, historians have carefully examined black culture, the slave personality, and the black family, and their conclusions about all three have evolved through several stages, each a reflection of the prevailing climate of opinion at the time.

During the first half-century after the Civil War, Americans were trying to cope with a number of problems, including industrialization, the "new immigration," and the rise of the city. The tensions associated with these changes helped popularize a host of racist theories. The publication of Charles Darwin's *Origin of Species* in 1859 inspired social scientists like Herbert Spencer and William Graham Sumner to apply the theory of natural selection to human society. This was Social Darwinism, the belief that certain people were genetically more "fit" than others and destined for success. At the same time, historians like George Bancroft and Herbert Baxter Adams, political scientists Francis Lieber and John W. Burgess, biologist Robert Knox, and classicist William F. Allen began promoting the theory of Teutonic origins, arguing that Anglo-Saxon, Nordic, and Germanic peoples were the superior race, responsible for free enterprise capitalism, political liberty, and technological progress. They also claimed that Jews, Slavs, Italians,

and Greeks, though "racially superior" to brown and especially black people, were nevertheless markedly inferior to Germans, Anglo-Saxons, and Scandinavians in intellectual capacity, ambition, and social organization.
A eugenics movement urging Anglo-Saxon, Nordic, and Germanic Protestants to marry among themselves and perpetuate the gene pool accompanied the racist propaganda.
These whites especially emphasized the inferiority of
Indians, Mexicans, Asians, and blacks, and their assumptions reached fruition in the reservation and allotment
systems, the acquisition of Mexican-American land, the
restrictions on Asian immigration, the decision of the
McKinley administration to establish an overseas empire
in 1898, and the appearance of Jim Crow laws throughout
the South.[1]

Prevailing views of blacks were the most hostile of
all. For nearly 250 years slavery had performed a dual
function in the United States--generating an endless
supply of cheap labor to the plantations and providing
whites with a form of absolute control over their increasingly large minority. The demise of slavery in 1865
had not only destroyed that guaranteed labor source but
had eliminated ownership as a means of social control.
To regain that control and keep blacks in the cotton
fields, southern whites had practically resurrected slavery in the form of poll taxes, literacy tests, grand-
father clauses, white primaries, sharecropping, debt
peonage, and Jim Crow laws. Early in the twentieth century, just as this new system of race relations was becoming complete, anti-black violence became more and more
common. The lynching of blacks increased dramatically
in the South, as did race riots in northern cities--New
York City in 1900; Springfield, Illinois, in 1906; East
St. Louis in 1917; and Chicago in 1919. The butt of
white jokes and white violence, black people were exper-
iencing one of their worst times in American history.

Not surprisingly, most historians looked at slavery
through that racist lens, imposing on the past the biases
of the present. Except for the black historian W. E. B.
DuBois, scholars saw blacks as a universally inferior
people, happy enough in a childlike way but incapable of
coping with life without close supervision. In project-
ing that prejudice back upon slavery, historians took an
extremely negative view of the slave personality, the
black family, and Afro American culture. They argued
that all slaves had been intellectually retarded and irresponsible; that all black families had been matriarchal
and dysfunctional, characterized by incompetent husbands
and parents unconcerned about their children's welfare;

24

and that Afro American culture had been non-existent, except as a crude and primitive way of expressing only the most base human needs. For two generations, the vast majority of Americans accepted this racist dogma.

In 1906 Albert B. Hart set the stage for the next generation of historians when he published *Slavery and Abolition, 1831-1841*. He wrote:

> The majority of the negroes were course and unattractive in appearance. Women were clumsy, awkward, gross, elephantine in all their movements, ... sly, sensual, and shameless in all their expressions and demeanor.[2]

> A slave was not to be trusted since they were prone to lying and stealing. At best they were thought big children, pleased with trifles and easily forgetful of penalties and pain.[3]

Slaves made no cultural contribution to American life because they came from such retarded cultural backgrounds. As for the slave family, blacks felt little or no obligation to their spouses and parent-child relationships were weak, victims of the casual sensuality so characteristic of African culture. For Hart, there were no redeeming qualities to black life. Other scholars followed his lead.

For its time, the work of Ulrich B. Phillips, *American Negro Slavery*, became the classic treatment of the "peculiar institution." Phillips had enormous influence on popular views of the black personality, and although some historians, like Eugene Genovese, have recently reconsidered Phillips's reputation and praised his economic conclusions, his view of the slave personality was clearly a product of early twentieth century racism. For Phillips, there was no doubt that the slaves were inferior people, victims of a weak African environment and weak personal genes. The African climate

> discourages ... mental effort of severe or sustained character, and the negroes have submitted to that prohibition through countless generations, with excellent grace.[4]

Blacks were little more than adult children, devoid of any significant cultural heritage, completely under the benevolent influence of their masters, and far better off here than they had ever been in Africa. The dominant personality characteristics of the slaves stood in sharp contrast to the behavioral patterns of white society. Phillips wrote that the slaves exhibited

an eagerness for society, music and merriment, a fondness
for display whether of person, dress, vocabulary or emo-
tion, a not flagrant sensuality, a receptiveness toward any
religion whose exercises were exhilirating, a proneness to
superstition, a courteous acceptance of subordination, an
avidity for praise, a readiness for loyalty of a feudal
sort, and ... a healthy human repugnance toward overwork...
the pickaninnies were winsome, and their parents, free of
expense and anxiety for their sustenance, could hardly have
had more of them than they wanted.[5]

Irresponsible and innocent, the slaves were basically a
happy people, free of the day-to-day anxieties of self-
support and free to give vent to their more physical
emotions. For Phillips, their African background and
their cultural heritage had suited them well to a life
of control and supervision. Benevolent and benign,
slavery was a paternalistic institution in the South.

   Because of his scholarly credentials as well as the
care he took in his research, Ulrich B. Phillips influenced nearly two generations of American historians. His
conclusions on the economic operation of the plantation
and the economics of slavery are still respected, but it
was his racism that became so glaringly apparent in the
next forty years of history textbooks. As late as 1937,
the historian James Randall wrote that in

   contrast to other races, the Negro adapted himself to bondage with a minimum of resistance, doing cheerfully the man-
   ual work of the South and loyally serving those who held
   him in bondage.[6]

Unfortunately, even the best of Phillips's research was
destined to fall into disrepute because the social attitudes upon which many of his conclusions rested were
changing. Even as an intellectual consensus was forming
around his work, the social and economic facts of life in
the United States were undermining it. The rise of a
black middle class was generating a demand for equality.
After the Civil War, the Freedmen's Bureau had set up
400 elementary and secondary schools for black children
in the South, and private philanthropists established
Howard University, Hampton Institute, St. Augustine's
College, Johnson C. Smith University, Atlanta University,
Storer College, and Fisk University for black students.
Over the years, as business people, journalists, clergy-
men, lawyers, teachers, physicians, nurses, and social
workers came out of the black colleges, a self-conscious
middle class appeared in the black community. Enjoying
relative economic security, they constantly compared

their segregation and discrimination with the egalitarian values of American culture.

At the same time, a new group of white liberals were beginning to demand that social justice be extended to blacks as well as whites. Early in the twentieth century, Oswald Garrison Villard, grandson of the abolitionist William Lloyd Garrison, called for black civil liberties; writers William Walling and William Dean Howells condemned racism; philosopher John Dewey protested Jim Crow laws; and social workers Jane Addams and Mary White Ovington demanded political and economic equality. These influential white liberals gave the young black civil rights movement respectability, and their joint efforts with prominent blacks like W. E. B. DuBois led to the creation of the National Association for the Advancement of Colored People in 1910.

Even more important in changing the prevailing climate of opinion about black people was the northern migration of southern blacks after 1914. Between 1870 and 1890 some 80,000 had moved out of the South, but between 1910 and 1920 the black population of the North increased from 850,000 to 1.4 million, and by 1930 to 2.3 million. Large black communities appeared throughout the Northeast and Midwest. During the 1930s most of them deserted the Republican Party, after seventy years of Civil War loyalty, and voted for Franklin D. Roosevelt. In the process, the urban blacks became a powerful force in the national Democratic Party, forcing more and more concessions to their civil rights demands. The northern migration also produced a black cultural revival known as the "Harlem Renaissance." Beginning in the 1920s, people like James Weldon Johnson, Claude McKay, Jean Turner, Countee Cullen, Langston Hughes, Richard Wright, Irving Miller, and Anne Spencer graphically portrayed the plight and promise of black people and protested discrimination. The prevailing image of black people as incompetent children began to break down. These black artists and scholars revitalized African pride and treated black culture neither as a mirror of white culture nor as a pathological reaction to racism, but as a fulfilling and functional way of interpreting reality and expressing needs. Under the pressures of the black middle class, the new black power in the Democratic Party, and the cultural expressions of black artists and writers, the traditional racist assumptions seemed less and less capable of offering any reasonable description of Afro American life. The long-held portrait of "happy darkies" ignorant of any heritage and oblivious to family needs and personal relationships began losing its credibility. On the eve

27

of World War II, as social and economic changes altered public attitudes, historians too began re-evaluating their own attitudes about the past.

There had been, of course, some isolated "voices in the wilderness" crying out against the consensus. A few scholars--George W. Williams in *A History of the Negro Race in America* (1883), W. E. B. DuBois in *The Souls of Black Folk* (1903), and Carter Woodson in *The African Background Outlined* (1936)--had been countering the racist consensus for years, but it was not until the late 1930s that real interpretive changes began appearing. A major change came in 1939 when the black sociologist E. Franklin Frazier wrote *The Negro Family in the United States*. Although some of his conclusions about Africa and the slave were similar to those of Hart and Phillips, his explanation for slave pathologies was quite different. Where the earlier historians had blamed slave problems on their race, Frazier clearly placed responsibility on white slaveowners and the oppressive nature of human bondage. He believed that the slaves had no cultural background; the horrors of the "Middle Passage," the dispersal of slaves throughout the South, and the mixing of African slaves with Afro American natives all diluted the African background until it had no influence on slave culture.

African traditions and practices did not take root and survive in the United States... Probably never before in history has a people been so nearly completely stripped of its social heritage as the Negroes who were brought to America.[7]

The slaves were cultural blanks upon their arrival, almost without a heritage, ready to be imbued with the benefits of western civilization. "As regards Negro family life," Franklin wrote, "there is no reliable evidence that African culture has had any influence on its development.[8] The black family was at the mercy of the American environment, and it deteriorated badly. Because the slave marriage was controlled by the white master and often disrupted by sale, family life tended to be impermanent, marked by casual feelings rather than true devotion. For Frazier, slave marriages were often the result of simple sexual lust, and easily dissolved when lust disappeared. Only when the slaves modeled their values after those of white society did their marriages acquire any maturity or any longevity. Relationships between husband and wife were very weak, as was the bond between parents and children. In that regard, black society was very different from white society, so black people were fundamentally different from whites.

28

Where the assimilation of Western mores went farthest and
the development of personality was highest, the organization of family life approached most closely the pattern
of white civilization. But in the end fundamental economic forces and material interests might shatter the
toughest bonds of familiar sentiments and parental love.[9]

Despite his own black heritage and his personal re-
pulsion for the institution of slavery, Frazier still
would only evaluate black family life in terms of white
culture. His indictment of black men was even stronger.
Emasculated of any patriarchal authority because of the
overwhelming power of the white master, black men became
weak and culturally impotent, with the black family taking on a decidedly maternal flavor. Worse still, the
pains of childbirth and the rigors of bondage disrupted
even the maternal instincts which some historians had
at least given black women credit for possessing.

Pregnancy and childbirth often meant only suffering for
the slave mother who, because of her limited contacts with
her young, never developed that attachment which grows out
of physiological and emotional responses to its needs...
where such limitations were placed upon the mother's spon-
taneous emotional responses to the needs of her children
and where even her suckling and fondling of them were restricted, it was not natural that she often showed little
attachment to her offspring.[10]

Like African culture, the slave family was a bankrupt
institution, incapable of providing emotional nourish-
ment to adults or emotional security to children. For
all of his hostility to slavery, Frazier had not painted
a very positive picture of black culture.

A major breakthrough in the scholarly treatment of
black culture came in 1941 as part of Gunnar Myrdal's
study of black life in the United States. Myrdal had
commissioned the historical anthropologist Melville J.
Herskovits to study the roots of black culture, and
Herskovits published *The Myth of the Negro Past* in 1941.
For Herskovits, much of the earlier work of historians
was badly misleading. He denied that "Negroes are vir-
ually of a childlike character, and adjust easily to
the most unsatisfactory social situations, which they
accept readily and even happily..."[11] He similarly rejected the claim that blacks did not have a past.[12]
Slaves were not childlike people content with bondage
but proud people who resisted slavery in subtle, nonvio-
lent ways as well as through open resistance. Nor had
they forgotten their African past. Indeed, African

traditions, attitudes, and institutions had survived the
Middle Passage, including techniques for cooking, birth-
ing, childrearing, and health care. Slaves adopted fundamental Protestantism but imbued it with an African emo
tional spirit, replete with African musical rhythms,
dances, voodooism, folk culture, and grave decorations.
Although the slaves spoke English, it was unique in pronunciation, grammar, and morphology. They placed English words in a grammatical context which was both English and African in origin. To argue that Africans, unlike other immigrants to the United States, had somehow
lost their culture was patently absurd to Herskovits.13

Two years later, the radical historian Herbert Aptheker wrote *American Negro Slave Revolts* and denied slave
infantilism and contentment. Instead of portraying millions of happy slaves laboring with love for their white
masters, Aptheker wrote of discontented slaves who escaped the drudgery and hopelessness of bondage through
sabotage, shamming illness, stealing, suicide, self-
mutilation, strikes, escape, and organized rebellion.
The idea that any human being could be happy while being
"beaten, branded, sold, degraded, denied a thousand and
one privileges they see enjoyed by others" was quite
ludicrous.14 For Aptheker, slaves were no different
than whites in their desire to be free.

Perhaps the most influential book in the revision of
the Afro American past came from the pen of Kenneth
Stampp in 1956. The appearance of *The Peculiar Institution. Slavery in the Antebellum South* coincided with th
birth of the modern civil rights movement and gained immediate popularity. Stampp's work was an open assault
on Ulrich B. Phillips, a denial of even the notion that
slaves were content with their bondage. When they did
exhibit childlike irresponsibility, it was merely drama,
a contrived act to beat the system.

> Slaves encouraged their masters to underrate their intelli-
> gence. Ignorance was a high virtue in human chattel. The
> master's purpose was to keep his slave in the state of ig-
> norance. Slaves were shrewd enough to make him think he
> had succeeded.15

Paternalistic masters demanded a childlike dependency,
and slaves displaying the least independence were the
most rewarded and the least suspect. Taking a cue from
Aptheker, Stampp argued that the slaves were actually a
"troublesome property," given to constant acts of clum-
siness, sabotage, laziness, feigned illness, escape,
revenge, and rebellion to express their loathing of

bondage. For Stampp, slavery was a dehumanizing and de-
grading institution, exactly the opposite of what Ulrich
Phillips had made it out to be.[16]

But at the same time, Stampp largely accepted the conclusions of E. Franklin Frazier on the nature of the
black family, similarly blaming the social pathologies
on white racism rather than on the African background.
The constant pressure of forced separation through sale
created extraordinary psychological pain and a certain
protective distance between family members. Because the
white master denied the black father any authority, most
children had no respect for their father and he had very
little influence in their lives. The legal system did
not recognize slave marriages and the plantation denied
any economic role to the slave family. Not surprisingly,
according to Stampp, slaves were weak and unstable, and
there

> was a casual attitude ... toward marriage ... the failure
> of any deep and enduring affection to develop between some
> husbands and wives ... the indifference with which most
> fathers and even some mothers regarded their children...
> the widespread sexual promiscuity of both men and women.[17]

The black family was the victim of "the peculiar institution."

Three years after the appearance of *The Peculiar Institution*, Stanley B. Elkins wrote *Slavery. A Problem
in American Intellectual and Institutional Life* (1959).
In an ironic twist, Elkins accepted Stampp's argument
that slavery was a brutalizing way of life while simul-
taneously accepting Phillips's claim that the slaves
were childlike in their behavior. For Elkins, the frequent descriptions of "Sambo" throughout the South were
too common to deny, so he accepted "Samboism" as a characteristic of the southern slave. He described the
"Sambo" slave as an emotionally weak adult afflicted
with a short attention span, low intelligence, childlike
dependency, and an unwitting sense of irresponsibility.
But where Phillips associated "Samboism" with genetically inherited patterns of behavior, and Stampp with simple cunning, Elkins traced it back to a personality
flaw. For years the sociological and psychological lit-
eratures had described concentration camp Jews in "Sam-
boesque" terms: weak, uncertain, dependent, and frightened children. Under such extraordinary pressures,
their personalities changed. In response to the total
authoritarianism of the Nazi SS, incarcerated Jews re-
verted to the "Sambo" personality:

31

> The concentration camp was not only a perverted slave sys-
> tem; it was also--what is less obvious but even more to
> the point--a perverted patriarchy... The role was per-
> vasive; it vetoed any other role and smashed all prior
> ones. Survivors had to play their roles well.[18]

After long periods, the forced role was transformed into
a personality trait, and Elkins argued that a similar
process operated on Afro American slaves. Like the concentration camp, the plantation was a closed system in
which power flowed in only one direction, from master to
slave. The white master expected all the qualities of a
child in his slaves.

> He might conceiveably have to expect in the child--his
> loyalty, docility, humility, cheerfulness, and his dili-
> gence--such additional qualities as irresponsibility,
> playfulness, silliness, laziness, and (quite possibly)
> tendencies to lying and stealing... Absolute power for
> the master meant absolute dependency for the slave--the
> dependency not of the developing child, but of the perpet-
> ual child.[19]

Victimized by absolute impotence in a closed society,
black slaves had been subtly and slowly changed into
"Sambos."

Although these scholars had come a long way from the
work of Albert Hart and Ulrich B. Phillips, particularly in their understanding of the dynamics of white racism, they had hardly at all transcended the general consensus about the slave family, slave personality, and
black culture. For Frazier and Stampp, the black family
was pathetically weak and disintegrated, marked by casual and impersonal relationships. For Elkins, the slave
personality was childlike and disturbed, incapable of
functioning with maturity. That these scholars had
blamed white society rather than black genes or the African background for the slave pathologies did not change
their generally negative conclusions about the nature of
black life. For all their liberalism--their rage over
racism and their guilt about the sins of the past--the
revisionists remained much in the mold set by an earlier
generation of white historians. The slave family, black
culture, and the slave personality were all abnormal and
pitiful.

This sympathetically negative view of the slave personality and the slave family was reinforced by their in-
ability to deal with black culture on its own terms.
Frazier had argued that the Africans came to America with

32

virtually no cultural baggage of their own, that they
basically became what whites made them. In what today
seems an extraordinarily naive statement, Stampp said,
with the righteous indignation of white liberalism,
that "innately Negroes are, after all, only white men
with black skins, nothing more, nothing less."20 He
measured all of black behavior in terms of white racism
and the economic dynamics of slavery, as if there was no
independent Afro American dimension to slave cultural
life. For Elkins, the "Sambo" personality, so common to
black life, was simply a pathological response to white
authoritarianism. The existence of a mature, functioning Afro American culture was hardly a consideration at
all; the liberal revisionists could not see beyond the
limits of white society. Slaves existed only in terms
of their relationships with their white masters.

But once again, social and economic changes in the
structure of American life were paving the way for a
more sophisticated interpretation of the slave personality, the slave family, and black culture. One day in
1955, Rosa Parks, tired after a long day of work, sat
down in a city bus in Montgomery, Alabama, and refused
to move to the back, where blacks were traditionally confined. Her decision set off a chain reaction in which
Montgomery blacks boycotted city buses and pushed the
system toward bankruptcy, demanding integration and more
black bus drivers. The leader of the boycott, a young
minister named Martin Luther King, Jr., rocketed to
national prominence as the boycotts spread to other
southern cities. From that beginning, right through the
"sit-ins" of 1960, the "freedom rides" of 1961, the gath-
ering of 250,000 people in Washington, D.C., in 1963,
the Civil Rights Act of 1964, the black rebellions in
Watts in 1965 and Newark and Detroit in 1967, and the
black power movement of people like Eldridge Cleaver and
Stokely Carmichael, whites had to confront an aggressive,
demanding Afro American community. Rather than simply
condemning antebellum racism and its effects, the scholars of the 1960s and 1970s had to deal with black culture
on its own terms, and the result has been a more sensi-
tive, integrated portrait of slave life.

Influenced by these changes in the American social
climate, a new generation of black and white historians--
Eugene Genovese, Peter H. Wood, Edmund Morgan, Leon F.
Litwack, John Blassingame, Leslie Owens, Gerald Mullin,
George Rawick, Herbert Gutman, Rogert Fogel, Stanley
Engerman, and Lawrence Levine--have drawn a startlingly
new and complex portrait of slave life. Except for the
earlier work of Herskovits, these scholars were the first

to accept black culture on its own terms rather than viewing it exclusively as a white derivative. Instead of denying the African background, they tended to view slave religion, language, and folk values as subtle blends of the African heritage and the American environment. Black culture was far more than what whites had made of it. As for the slave personality, it was not a warped emotionalism based on forced infantilism. Instead, they argued that there was no "slave personality" explaining all black behavior. Indeed, the personalities of the slaves were complex and varied, dependent on individual differences as well as the behavior of white owners and overseers. Finally, they discarded the consensus that the black family was weak, temporary, and impersonal, arguing that the black family under slavery, despite all the pressures, was a healthy institution fulfilling the needs of its individual members.

John W. Blassingame, in *The Slave Community. Plantation Life in the Antebellum South* (1972), argued that African culture survived the enslavement process, and that Old World musical rhythms, language, folk medicine, folk tales, family values, and religious superstitions blended gently into Afro American culture, giving slaves the tools to survive emotionally the rigors of bondage. For Blassingame, the

> most remarkable aspect of the whole process of enslavement is the extent to which the American-born slaves were able to retain their ancestors' culture... Antebellum black slaves created several unique cultural forms which lightened their burden of oppression, promoted group solidarity, provided ways for verbalizing aggression, sustaining hope, building self-esteem, and often represented areas of life largely free from the control of whites.[21]

In the slave quarters, away from the pressure and supervision of whites, black culture thrived, fostering a sense of cooperation, mutual assistance, and racial solidarity. In a direct rejection of the "Sambo" thesis, Blassingame argued that slaves survived the horrors of bondage "without becoming abjectly docile, infantile, or submissive."[22] When masters were terribly harsh, patterns of docility prevailed in his presence. Some blacks lost feelings of self-worth, some wished to be white, and some fled to freedom to avoid cruelty. But most of them balanced "on a tight rope between revealing their true character and incurring the anger of whites, and masking their feelings and surviving."[23]

In *Flight and Rebellion. Slave Resistance in Eighteenth-Century Virginia* (1972), Gerald W. Mullin pointed

out the weaknesses in earlier approaches to slave life.
The scholarly debate over

> the extent to which slaves "accomodated" to a "system"
> characterized as a type of "total" institution ... is
> anachronistic; it views rebellious slaves out of their
> historical context ... concentrating on the whites and
> the structural features of the institutions they created.24

In analyzing the patterns of slave resistance, Mullin
focused on the interplay between African and colonial
English cultures, arguing that the nature of slave rebelliousness was a function of acculturation to American
society as well as types of employment. As a slave began to learn English, familiarize himself with white
ways, and acquire job skills, he became more externally-
oriented, more likely to direct his rebellion at the
goal of freedom by outright escape. Less acculturated
slaves were rebellious too, but their resistance was
inner-oriented, taking the forms of sullenness and destruction of property. In terms of occupation, slaves
with skills and semi-skills who were able to travel away
from the fields and plantation house became even more
acculturated and more committed to freedom, more indiv-
idualistic, and more outwardly rebellious. The great
irony of southern life, Mullin observed, was that the
white desire to rapidly acculturate their slaves, in the
name of labor efficiency and profit, only made slaves
more outwardly rebellious and more difficult to control.

The emphasis on black culture also appeared in George
P. Rawick's *From Sundown to Sunup: The Making of the
Black Community* (1972). Taking his cue from Chapter Two
("From Day Clean to First Dark") of Stampp's *The Peculiar
Institution*, Rawick argued that the essence of black culture was outside the occupational relationship because
blacks then were always in the presence of whites. It
was only after work, away from whites in the slave quarters, that black culture really manifested itself. Life
from sundown to sunup allowed the slaves to live for
themselves, to express their frustrations and draw support from one another. Rejecting the earlier notion of
casual and impersonal family relationships, Rawick
claimed that slave marriages were strong, and when parents, children, or spouses were separated through sale,
the black community became an extended family where all
adults looked after one another and the children. For
Rawick, "Family life enabled the slave to develop black
pride, black identity, black culture, the black community, and black rebellion in America."25 Indeed, the en-
tire structure of the black community was designed to

institutionalize the various forms of rebellion as well as to provide the emotional support every slave needed to deal with lifetime bondage.

Eugene D. Genovese, in *Roll, Jordan, Roll: The World the Slaves Made* (1974), magnified that focus on the slave community by interpreting plantation life as a symbiotic cultural relationship between whites and most blacks. Using a form of social Marxism, Genovese created an image of a rather monolithic slave community. Slave life and black culture were remarkably consistent from plantation to plantation, regardless of the size of the farming operation, the number of slaves there, its location in the upper or lower South, or its economic profitability. In terms of conscious identity, there were no major differences between field hands and house servants, full-bloods or mulattoes, and native- or African-born slaves. Nor did slaves separate themselves into groups of accomodationists or rebels. Loyalty, accomodation, obedience, and rebelliousness were all part of a single continuum resting upon the paternalistic relationship between the white ruling class and the enslaved workers. For Genovese, plantation life revolved around a system of mutually reinforcing obligations between masters and slaves. Whites viewed themselves as paternalistic masters offering sustenance and protection to their dependent slaves, and they expected loyalty and gratitude in return. The slaves, by fulfilling their work obligation, earned their "rights": decent food, garden plots, adequate clothing, fair discipline, and most importantly, the right to privacy in the quarters where they could develop a cultural autonomy and sense of community. By developing this sense of rights, they emotionally and intellectually rejected the idea of slavery.

> To this tendency of making themselves creatures of another's will, they counterposed a tendency to assert themselves as autonomous human beings ... slaves acted consciously and unconsciously to transform paternalism into a doctrine of protection of their own rights--a doctrine that represented the negation of the idea of slavery itself.[26]

With that sense of independence, the slaves created a cultural world of their own. By spiritually emancipating the individual slave, black religion generated a communalism which paved the way for the emergence of a collective black consciousness. Religion became the emotional center of black life. While offering an other-worldly escape for some and a form of millenial protest for others, black religion

gave the slaves the one thing they absolutely had to have
if they were to resist being transformed into the Sambos
they had been programmed to become. It fired them with a
sense of their own worth before God and man. It enabled
them to prove to themselves, and to a world that never
ceased to need reminding, that no man's will can become
that of another unless he himself wills it--that the
ideal of slavery cannot be realized, no matter how badly
the body is broken and the spirit tormented.[27]

The slave family was as important to black religion in
the emotional life of the community. Genovese plain-
tively asked what evidence it would take to "convince
skeptics that the essential story of black men in slavery lay with the many who overcame every possible hard-
ship and humiliation to stand fast to their families."[28]
Instead of matriarchies, the slaves valued two-parent,
male-centered households.

If many men lived up to their assigned irresponsibility,
others, probably a majority, overcame all obstacles and
provided a positive male image for their wives and children... A remarkable number of women did everything possible to strengthen their men's self-esteem and to defer
to their leadership. What has usually been viewed as a
debilitating female supremacy was in fact a closer ap-
proximation to a healthy sexual equality than was possible
for whites...[29]

To an absolute storm of protest in 1974, Robert W.
Fogel and Stanley L. Engerman published their book *Time
on the Cross. The Economics of American Negro Slavery*.
Fogel and Engerman focused most of their attention on
the economics of slavery and reached what many historians considered outrageous conclusions: that slavery was
a highly profitable system for the South; slavery was
thriving economically on the eve of the Civil War; slave
agriculture was more efficient than free agriculture;
the material conditions of slaves was equal to or better
than that of free industrial workers; and that over the
course of a lifetime each slave managed to keep about 90
percent of the income he produced.[30] In that sense,
Fogel and Engerman seemed to be writing from the perspective of the earlier racist historians like Albert Hart
and Ulrich B. Phillips, except that by arguing that slavery was essentially a benign institution, they denied
that it emasculated the black male and destroyed the
black family. For Fogel and Engerman, the "typical
field hand was not lazy, inept, and unproductive. On
average he was harder-working and more efficient than
his white counterpart" because white masters used a very

37

complex system of rewards and punishments.[31] Fogel and
Engerman also argued that stories of slave-breeding and
sexual exploitation, as well as forced sales, were highly exaggerated, so the black family did not suffer from
them.

> The belief that slave-breeding, sexual exploitation, and
> promiscuity destroyed the black family is a myth. The
> family was the basic unit of social organization under
> slavery. It was to the economic interest of planters to
> encourage the stability of slave families and most of
> them did so...[32]

Black mothers loved their children, black fathers were
the heads of the home, and the black family was central
to black culture, not because the family was strong
enough to withstand white brutality but because white
brutality did not exist on an extensive scale.

Building on the accumulating consensus, Peter H. Wood
wrote *Black Majority. Negroes in Colonial South Carolina
from 1670 through the Stono Rebellion* in 1974. Wood argued quite convincingly that the slaves had retained
much of their African background during the colonial
period, and that whites actually recruited slaves from
certain parts of Africa because of their economic exper-
tise. South Carolina whites prized slaves from the
Gambia River because they were expert horsemen and herds-
men. Blacks from the Congo-Angola region were responsible for teaching whites the art of planting, harvesting,
and cooking the rice which became the South Carolina
staple. Many Africans were also familiar with indigo
and cotton cultivation. The use of Palmetto leaves as
fans and brooms, gourds and calabashes as pails, drugging
a pond to kill and catch fish, and use of alligators to
protect livestock were all African-based. Finally,
Wood made a strong connection between the Gullah dialect
and the emergence of black English.

Wood also argued that in South Carolina, where blacks
were the majority,

> there existed the "critical mass" necessary for preserving
> and synthesizing traditions of behavior, speech, and myth.
> There was a tendency toward social, and occasionally eco-
> nomic, self-sufficiency among blacks as their numbers ex-
> panded. A voluntary separation from the white community
> went along with denser population, wider contacts, and
> increasingly independent living quarters.[33]

Early in the eighteenth century, the demand for labor in

South Carolina, especially skilled labor, was so great that slaves were able to improve their economic situation. As fisherman, herders, farmers, and craftsmen, slaves became quite enterprising, even selling many products on the "black market." Incentives for hard work were quite real. But as the black population increased, so did white anxiety and political controls, and as white controls tightened, black resistance became stronger.

It is not surprising that slaves responded to these pressures in a wide variety of ways. To separate their reactions into docility on the one hand and rebellion on the other ... is to underestimate the complex nature of the contradictions each Negro felt in the face of new provocations and new penalties. It is more realistic to think in terms of a spectrum of response, ranging from complete submission to total resistance, along which any given individual could be located at any given time.[34]

In 1976 Leslie Howard Owens, in *This Species of Property. Slave Life and Culture in the Old South*, agreed with Wood that the idea of "Sambo" as a plantation type was very difficult to accept because slaves adapted to the situations at hand. Though no doubt present on some plantations as a real personality type, Samboism was the exception rather than the rule, and that varieties of resistance to slavery was a more realistic model for slave life. Owen was quite convinced that historians had generally underestimated the extent of slave rebelliousness. Fathers were responsible heads of families, improving their families' welfare at every opportunity by planting vegetables, hunting, and stealing. As for black culture, it reached its greatest expression in the black church, where slaves reshaped their lives and found depth and purpose.[35]

The black family, for Herbert Gutman in *The Black Family in Slavery and Freedom, 1750-1925* (1976), was the essence of black culture. African religious, folk, family, and cultural practices came across the Atlantic with the slaves, but by 1800, when American-born blacks outnumbered Africans, a new Afro American culture had emerged. Acculturation was a complex process, evolving through four stages, and the black family developed into the foundation of black culture. Men and women remained together as a family unit during slavery and after emancipation; in fact, the widespread migration of former slaves during the late 1860s was not a manifestation of genetic irresponsibility as some historians once argued, but a desperate attempt to locate husbands, wives, parents, and children sold away from their families. Marriage and family relationships were certainly strained by sale and the threat of sale, so slaves socialized themselves and their children to prepare emotionally for the possibility. To survive the grief of separation and to perpetuate the culture, slaves developed a communal, extended family mentality, where practically all adults were "aunts" or "uncles" to all the children of the quarters. The extended family network immediately incorporated all new arrivals to the plantation. Gutman also argued that most slaves lived in two-parent households where marriages survived over long periods of time. That slaves placed great value on the formal commitment implied by marriage is quite clear from the large numbers of them who registered their marriages in county courthouses throughout the South after emancipation. Most slave households were also patriarchal, where children traced their names back through their father's ancestry and where major household decisions were made by men. Proud and emotionally healthy, the slave family nurtured feelings of self-worth for men, women, and children.

If Gutman's work defined the black family, it was the publication of Lawrence W. Levine's *Black Culture and Black Consciousness. Afro-American Folk Thought from Slavery to Freedom* in 1977 which first exposed the internal dynamics of the slave mind. Relying on the orally transmitted culture of Afro Americans--songs, folk tales, proverbs, aphorisms, jokes, verbal games, and narrative poems--Levine explained how the slaves forged a rich value system out of the African past and the American present. During the era of slavery, black cosmology was a holistic one, viewing man, God, and the environment as inseparable parts of the sacred world. He could not tolerate the traditional view of black history as a story of total degradation and suffering.

> Even in the midst of the brutalities and injustices ...
> black men and women were able to find the means to sustain
> a far greater degree of self-pride and group cohesion than
> the system they lived under even intended for them to be
> able to do so ... they formed and maintained kinship net-
> works, made love, raised and socialized children, built
> a religion, and created a rich expressive culture in which
> they articulated their feelings and hopes and dreams.36

Black culture was hardly a copy of white values. Indeed, it was quite distinct, and that very uniqueness permitted slaves to psychologically isolate themselves from the cultural system which was oppressing them. By

maintaining a distinct consciousness and a separate identity, the slaves actually made sure that the Sambo personality did not become a pattern of black behavior.

> The slaves' expressive arts and sacred beliefs were more
> than merely a series of outlets or strategies; they were
> instruments of life, of sanity, of health, and of self-
> respect. Slave music, slave religion, slave folk beliefs--
> the entire sacred world of the black slaves--created the
> necessary space between the slaves and their owners and
> were the means of preventing legal slavery from becoming
> spiritual slavery.[37]

Unlike Fogel and Engerman, who had tied the stability of
slave society to the benevolent nature of white slavery,
Levine too claimed that slaves were resilient survivors,
able to generate feelings of community and individual
self-worth despite the trauma of bondage.

The most recent contribution to the historiography of
slave society is Leon F. Litwack's *Been in the Storm So
Long. The Aftermath of Slavery* (1979). Litwack chose
to analyze the slave personality, slave family, and black
culture by focusing on the reaction of southern blacks
to the demise of the peculiar institution during and just
after the Civil War. Litwack quickly discarded any notions of Sambo and confirmed Genovese's thesis that slavery was a symbiotic relationship between whites and
blacks, with blacks conscious of their "rights." Despite
their so-called loyalty to their masters, they were un-
willing to surrender any privileges because of wartime
shortages, such as Saturday-night dances, the annual
barbecue, the supper expected after a slave wedding, or
Christmas holiday festivities. Litwack also agreed with
Leslie Howard Owen and Peter H. Wood that slaves responded to their masters with a wide range of feelings.
When whites lost loved ones in the conflict, some slaves
shared their grief while others were overjoyed at their
master's pain. The legend of slave docility was just
that, for in the absence of white men, slave resistance
and disaffection increased. Most of them welcomed the
Yankee soldiers with open arms and thrilled at the pros-
pect of freedom, defying the stereotype of the happy,
loyal slave. Gutman's argument on the stability of the
slave family was similarly confirmed by the slave pas-
sion for reuniting loved ones after the war. As late
as the 1880s in black and southern publications, former
slaves were still placing advertisements hoping to locate
loved ones sold away from them before 1865. Independent,
proud, and thrilled to be free, black people readily discarded bondage and began to reconstruct their lives in

the context of liberty.

Although historians have engaged in a great deal of scholarly debate during the last fifteen years over the "peculiar institution," a new consensus has nevertheless emerged concerning the personalities, family life, and cultural values of the American slaves. The older arguments of Albert Hart, Ulrich B. Phillips, and others that slaves were a racially inferior, rootless but happy people have been destroyed, as have the descriptions of black pathologies so central to the work of Kenneth Stampp, E. Franklin Frazier, and Stanley B. Elkins. The history of slavery is now seen in a very different light. Although some of the slaves no doubt responded to bondage with docile acquiescence and others with outright violence, most worked out their lives in a tenuous reciprocity with the white people who were dependent upon them, giving and taking as the individual occasion required. At the same time, back in the quarters, they were creating a unique blend of African and American customs and values, a new culture which separated and saved them from white society, and they were nurturing a rich family life which provided them with love, affection, and emotional security.

FOOTNOTES

[1] See James S. Olson, *The Ethnic Dimension in American History* (New York, 1979), pp. 210-213.

[2] Albert B. Hart, *Slavery and Abolition, 1831-1841* (New York, 1906), p. 93.

[3] *Ibid.*

[4] Ulrich B. Phillips, *American Negro Slavery* (New York, 1918), p. 4.

[5] *Ibid.*, pp. 291, 298.

[6] James Randall, *The Civil War and Reconstruction* (New York, 1937), p. 48. For the typical view of Africans as people without a past, see Robert E. Park, "The Conflict and Fusion of Cultures with Special Reference to the Negro," *Journal of Negro History*, 4(Spring, 1919), 116-118. For other works in the general tradition of Phillips, see Charles Sydnor, *Slavery in Mississippi* (Baton Rouge, 1933) and Ralph Flanders, *Plantation Slavery in Georgia* (Chapel Hill, 1933).

[7]E. Franklin Frazier, *The Negro Family in the United States* (Chicago, 1939), pp. 7-8, 21.

[8]*Ibid.*, p. 12.

[9]*Ibid.* p. 41.

[10]*Ibid.*, pp. 48, 61.

[11]Melville J. Herskovits, *The Myth of the Negro Past* (Chicago, 1941), p. 1.

[12]*Ibid.*, p. 2.

[13]*Ibid.*

[14]Herbert Aptheker, *American Negro Slave Revolts* (New York, 1943), p. 141.

[15]Kenneth M. Stampp, *The Peculiar Institution. Slavery in the Antebellum South* (New York, 1956), p. 99.

[16]*Ibid.*, pp. 86-140.

[17]*Ibid.*, pp. 345-346. For several other books in the Stampp tradition, see James Benson Sellers, *Slavery in Alabama* (University, Ala., 1950); Lorenzo Johnston Greene, *The Negro in Colonial New England, 1620-1776* (New York, 1942); Robert McColley, *Slavery and Jeffersonian Virginia* (Urbana, 1964); Orville W. Taylor, *Negro Slavery in Arkansas* (Durham, N.C., 1958); Joe Gray Taylor, *Negro Slavery in Louisiana* (Baton Rouge, 1963); Julia Floyd Smith, *Slavery and Plantation Growth in Antebellum Florida, 1821-1860* (Gainesville, 1973); and Richard Wade, *Slavery in the Cities* (New York, 1964).

[18]Stanley B. Elkins, *Slavery. A Problem in American Intellectual and Institutional Life* (Chicago, 1959), pp. 104, 126.

[19]*Ibid.*, pp. 126, 130.

[20]Stampp, *The Peculiar Institution*, p. vii.

[21]John H. Blassingame, *The Slave Community. Plantation Life in the Antebellum South* (New York, 1972), pp. 39, 41.

[22]*Ibid.*, p. 39.

[23]*Ibid.*, p. 209.

[24]Gerald W. Mullin, *Flight and Rebellion. Slave Resistance in Eighteenth-Century Virginia* (New York, 1972), p. 35.

[25]George P. Rawick, *From Sundown to Sunup: The Making of the Slave Community* (Westport, 1972), p. 93.

[26]Eugene D. Genovese, *Roll, Jordan, Roll: The World the Slaves Made* (New York, 1974), pp. 49, 91.

[27]*Ibid.*, p. 283.

[28]*Ibid.*, pp. 485-486.

[29]*Ibid.*, p. 500. Also see Robert S. Starobin, *Industrial Slavery in the Old South* (New York, 1970); Ronald L. Lewis, *Coal, Iron, and Slaves: Industrial Slavery in Maryland and Virginia, 1715-1865* (Westport, 1979); and Albert J. Raboteau, *Slave Religion: The "Invisible Institution" in the Antebellum South* (New York, 1978).

[30]Robert W. Fogel and Stanley L. Engerman, *Time on the Cross. The Economics of American Negro Slavery* (Boston, 1974), pp. 4-6.

[31]*Ibid.*, p. 5.

[32]*Ibid.*, pp. 127-141. For the scholarly criticism of Fogel and Engerman, see Paul David, *et al.*, *Reckoning With Slavery* (New York, 1976).

[33]Peter H. Wood, *Black Majority. Negroes in Colonial South Carolina from 1670 to the Stono Rebellion* (New York, 1974), p. 195.

[34]*Ibid.*, p. 285. Also see Daniel C. Littlefield, *Rice and Slavery. Ethnicity and the Slave Trade in Colonial South Carolina* (Baton Rouge, 1981).

[35]Leslie Howard Owen, *This Species of Property. Slave Life and Culture in the Old South* (New York, 1976), p. 41.

[36]Lawrence W. Levine, *Black Culture and Black Consciousness. Afro-American Folk Thought from Slavery to Freedom* (New York, 1977), p. xi.

[37]*Ibid.*, p. 80. For other discussions of the African background of slave culture, see S. W. Mintz, "Toward an Afro-American History," *The Journal of World History*, 13

(Summer, 1971), 317-332; As for the meaning of slavery in American life, see Edmund S. Morgan, *American Slavery, American Freedom. The Ordeal of Colonial Virginia* (New York, 1975); Winthrop Jordan, *White Over Black. American Attitudes Toward the Negro 1550-1812* (Chapel Hill, 1969); and David Brion Davis, *The Problem of Slavery in the Age of Revolution: 1770-1823* (Ithaca, 1975).

Chapter 3
Some Primary Sources

SLAVE NARRATIVES

Adams, John Quincy. *Narrative of The Life of John Quincy Adams, When in Slavery, and Now as a Freeman*. Harrisburg: 1872.

Aleckson, Sam. *Before the War, and After The Union*. Boston: 1929.

Allen, Richard. *The Life, Experience, And Gospel Labors of the Rt. Reverend Richard Allen*. Philadelphia: 1887.

Anderson, John. *The Story of the Life of John Anderson, A Fugitive Slave*. London: 1863.

Anderson, Robert. *From Slavery to Affluence*. Hemingford, Neb.: 1827.

Anderson, Solena. "Back in 'Dem Days': A Black Family Reminisces." *Journal of Mississippi History*, 36 (May, 1974).

Arter, Jared M. *Echoes From A Pioneer Life*. Atlanta: 1922.

Ball, Charles. *Slavery in the United States: A Narrative of the Life and Adventures of Charles Ball*. Lewiston, Pa.: 1836.

Bailey, David Thomas. "A Divided Prism: Two Sources of Black Testimony on Slavery." *Journal of Southern History*, 46 (August, 1980).

Banks, J. H. *A Narrative of Events Of The Life of J.H. Banks*. Liverpool: 1861.

Bayley, Solomon. *A Narrative of Some Remarkable Incidents, In the Life of Solomon Bayley, Formerly A Slave*. London: 1825.

Bibb, Henry. *Narrative of the Life and Adventures of Henry Bibb, An American Slave*. New York: 1849.

Black, Leonard. *The Life And Sufferings Of Leonard Black, A Fugitive From Slavery*. New Bedford: 1847.

Blassingame, John W., ed. *Slave Testimony: Letters, Speeches, Interviews, and Autobiographies, 1738-1938*. Baton Rouge: 1977.

Bontemps, Arna, ed. *Great Slave Narratives*. Boston: 1969.

Botkin, B. A. *Lay My Burden Down: A Folk History of Slavery*. Chicago: 1945.

Bratton, Mary J., ed. "Field's Observations: The Slave Narrative of a Nineteenth Century Virginian." *Virginia Magazine of History*, 88 (January, 1980).

Brown, Henry Box. *Narrative of Henry Box Brown*. Boston: 1851.

Brown, John. *Slave Life in Georgia*. London: 1855.

Brown, William Wells. *Narrative of William W. Brown, A Fugitive Slave*. Boston: 1847.

_____. *My Southern Home*. Boston: 1880.

Bruce, Henry Clay. *The New Man. Twenty-Nine Years a Slave. Twenty-Nine Years A Free Man*. York: 1895.

Burton, Annie L. *Memories of Childhood's Slavery Days*. Boston: 1909.

Butterfield, Stephen. *Black Autobiography in America*. Amherst: 1974.

Cade, John B. "Out of the Mouths of Ex-Slaves." *Journal of Negro History*, 20 (July, 1935).

Campbell, Israel. *An Autobiography*. Philadelphia: 1861.

Clarke, Lewis G. *Narrative of the Sufferings of Lewis Clarke*. Boston: 1845.

Cook, Charles Orson and James M. Poteet, eds. "'Dem Was Black Times Sure Nough': The Slave Narratives of Lydia Jefferson and Stephen Williams." *Louisiana History*, 20 (Summer, 1979).

Craft, William. *Running A Thousand Miles For Freedom: Or The Escape of William and Ellen Craft From Slavery*. London: 1860.

Curtin, Philip D., ed. *Africa Remembered: Narratives by West Africans from the Era of the Slave Trade*. Madison: 1968.

Davis, Noah. *A Narrative of The Life of Rev. Noah Davis, A Colored Man*. Baltimore: 1859.

Delaney, Lucy Ann. *From The Darkness Cometh The Light: Or Struggles For Freedom*. St. Louis: n.d.

Douglass, Frederick. *My Bondage and My Freedom*. New York: 1855.

_____. *The Narrative of Frederick Douglass*. New York: 1845.

Egypt, Ophelia, J. Masuoka, and Charles S. Johnson, eds. *The Unwritten History of Slavery: Autobiographical Accounts of Negro Ex-Slaves*. Nashville, Tenn.: 1945.

Escott, Paul D. *Slavery Remembered: A Record of Twentieth Century Slave Narratives*. Chapel Hill: 1979.

Feldstein, Stanley. *Once a Slave: The Slaves' View of Slavery*. New York: 1971.

Gifford, James M. "Black Hope and Despair in Antebellum Georgia: The William Moss Correspondence." *Prologue*, 8 (Fall, 1976).

Grandy, Moses. *Narrative of The Life of Moses Grandy*. London: 1843.

Gray, Thomas R. *The Confessions of Nat Turner*. Baltimore: 1831.

Green, Elisha W. *Life Of The Rev. Elisha W. Green*. Maysville, Ky.: 1888.

Green, William. *Narrative Of Events In The Life Of William Green*. Springfield: 1853.

Grimes, William. *Life of William Grimes, The Runaway Slave, Brought Down To The Present Time*. New Haven: 1855.

Hall, Samuel. *47 Years A Slave*. Washington, Iowa: 1912.

Harrison, Lowell H. "Memoirs of Slavery Days in Kentucky." *Filson Club Historical Quarterly*, 47 (July, 1973).

_____. "Recollections of Some Tennessee Slaves." *Tennessee Historical Quarterly*, 33 (Summer, 1974).

Heard, William H. *From Slavery To The Bishopric In The A. M. E. Church: An Autobiography*. Philadelphia: 1924.

Henson, Josiah. *The Life of Josiah Henson*. Boston: 1849.

_____. *Father Henson's Story of His Own Life.* New York: 1858.

Holsey, Lucius H. *Autobiography, Sermons, Addresses, And Essays.* Atlanta: 1898.

Hughes, Louis. *Thirty Years A Slave.* Milwaukee: 1897.

Jackson, Andrew. *Narrative and Writings of Andrew Jackson.* Syracuse: 1847.

Jamison, Monroe F. *Autobiography and Work of Bishop M. F. Jamison, D.D.* Nashville: 1912.

Jefferson, Isaac. *Life of Isaac Jefferson of Petersburg, Virginia, Blacksmith.* Charlottesville: 1951.

Johnson, Charles S. *Shadow of the Plantation.* Chicago: 1934.

Johnson, Thomas L. *Twenty-Eight Years A Slave: Or The Story Of My Life In Three Continents.* London: 1909.

Jones, Thomas. *The Experience of Thomas Jones, Who Was A Slave For Forty-Three Years.* Boston: 1850.

Keckley, Elizabeth. *Behind The Scenes.* New York: 1868.

Lane, Isaac. *Autobiography.* Nashville: 1916.

Lane, Lunsford. *The Narrative of Lunsford Lane.* Boston: 1848.

Langston, John Mercer. *From The Virginia Plantation To The National Capital.* Hartford: 1894.

Levstik, Frank J. "From Slavery to Freedom: Two Wartime Letters by One of the Conflict's Few Black Medal Winners." *Civil War Times Illustrated,* 11 (November, 1972).

Lewis, J. Vance. *Out of the Ditch.* Houston: 1910.

Loguen, Jermain Wesley. *The Rev. J. W. Loguen, As A Slave And As A Freedman.* Syracuse: 1859.

Lowery, I. E. *Life on the Old Plantation in Ante-Bellum Days: Or A Story Based on Facts.* Columbia, S.C.: 1911.

Marrs, Elijah P. *Life and History.* Louisville: 1885.

Mason, Isaac. *Life Of Isaac Mason As A Slave.* Worcester, Mass.: 1893.

Moore, John Hebron, ed. "A Letter from a Fugitive Slave." *Journal of Mississippi History,* 24 (April, 1855.

Newton, A. H. *Out of the Briars.* Philadelphia: 1910.

Northrup, Solomon. *Twenty Years A Slave*. London: 1853.

Nichols, Charles H. *Many Thousand Gone*. Leiden: 1963.

Offley, G. W. *A Narrative of the Life and Labors of the Rev. G. W. Offley, A Colored Man*. Hartford: 1860.

O'Neal, William. *Life and History of William O'Neal*. St. Louis: 1896.

Osofsky, Gilbert, ed. *Puttin' on Ole Massa*. New York: 1969.

Parker, Allen. *Recollections of Slavery Times*. Worcester: 1895.

Pennington, James W. C. *The Fugitive Blacksmith*. London: 1849.

Randolph, Peter. *Sketches of Slave Life*. Boston: 1855.

Rawick, George P. *The American Slave: A Composite Autobiography*. 19 vols. Westport: 1972.

Roberts, James. *The Narrative of James Roberts*. Hattiesburg: 1858.

Robinson, W. H. *From Log Cabin To The Pulpit*. Eau Clare: 1913.

Roper, Moses. *A Narrative of the Adventures and Escape of Moses Roper from American Slavery*. London: 1840.

Slotkin, Richard. "Narratives of Negro Crime in New England, 1675-1800." *American Quarterly*, 25 (March, 1973).

Smith, Amanda. *An Autobiography*. Chicago: 1893.

Smith, Venture. *A Narrative of the Life and Adventures of Venture, A Native of Africa*. New London: 1798.

Stanley, Linda. "James Carter's Account of His Sufferings in Slavery." *Pennsylvania Magazine of History and Biography*, 105 (July, 1981).

Starobin, Robert S. *Blacks in Bondage: Letters of American Slaves*. New York: 1974.

Steward, Austin. *Twenty-Two Years A Slave, And Forty Years A Freeman*. Rochester: 1861.

Stoyer, Jacob. *My Life in the South*. Salem: 1890.

Thompson, John. *The Life of John Thompson, A Fugitive Slave*. Worcester: 1856.

Vassa, Gustavus. *The Interesting Narrative of the Life of Olaudah Equiano, or Gustavus Vassa, The African.* London: 1794.

Veney, Bethany. *The Narrative of Bethany Veney, A Slave Woman.* Worcester: 1889.

Washington, Booker T. *Up From Slavery.* Cambridge: 1928.

Watkins, James. *Narrative of the Life of James Watkins.* Bolton, Eng.: 1852.

Watson, A. B., Paul Radin, and Charles S. Johnson, eds. *God Struck Me Dead: Religious Conversion Experiences of Ex-Slaves.* Nashville: 1945.

Webb, William. *The History of William Webb.* Detroit: 1873.

White, George. *A Brief Account Of The Life, Experience, Travels, and Gospel Labours Of George White, An African.* New York: 1810.

Wilkerson, James. *Wilkerson's History of His Travels & Labors, In the United States.* Columbus: 1861.

Williams, Isaac D. *Sunshine and Shadow of Slave Life.* East Saginaw: 1885.

Yetman, Norman R., ed. *Life Under the "Peculiar Institution": Selections from the Slave Narrative Collection.* New York: 1970.

TRAVEL ACCOUNTS

Adby, E. S. *Journal of a Residence and Tour in the United States of North America.* London: 1835.

Alexander, James Edward. *Transatlantic Sketches.* London: 1833.

Anburey, Thomas. *Travels Through the Interior Parts of America.* London: 1789.

Ashworth, Henry. *Tour in the United States.* London: 1861.

Baxter, W. E. *America and the Americans.* London: 1855.

Benwell, J. *An Englishman's Travels in America.* London: 1853.

Birkbeck, Morris. *Notes on a Journey to America.* Philadelphia: 1817.

Boucher, Jonathan. *Reminiscences.* Boston: 1923.

Bremer, Fredrika. *Homes of the New World.* New York: 1853.

Brickwell, John. *The Natural History of North Carolina.*
Dublin: 1737.

Candler, Isaac. *A Summary View of America.* London:
1824.

Chastellux, Francis Jean. *Travels in North America in
the Years 1780, 1781, and 1782.* Chapel Hill: 1963.

Daubney, Charles. *Journal of A Tour Through The United
States, and Canada, Made During the Years 1837-38.*
Oxford: 1843.

Davis, John. *Travels in the United States of America,
1798 to 1802.* Boston: 1910.

De Montule, Edouard. *Travels in America, 1816-1817.*
Bloomington: 1950.

Drayton, John. *A View of South Carolina.* 1802.

Easterby, J. H., ed. "South Carolina Through New Eng-
land Eyes: Almira Coffin's Visit to the Low
Country in 1851." *South Carolina Historical and
Genealogical Magazine,* 45 (July, 1944).

Eddis, William. *Letters from America, Historical and
Descriptive Comprising Occurrences from 1769 to
1777, Inclusive.* London: 1792.

Evarts, Jeremiah. *Through the South and West.* Lewis-
burg: 1956.

Faux, William. *Memorable Days in America.* London:
1823.

Feltman, William. *The Journal of Lieut. William Feltman
of the First Pennsylvania Regiment, 1781-82.*
Philadelphia: 1853.

Ferguson, William. *America by River and Rail.* London:
1856.

Finch, John. *Travels in the United States of America
and Canada.* London: 1833.

Glen, James. *A Description of South Carolina.* London:
1761.

Hall, Basil. *Travels in North America in the Years 1827
and 1828.* Philadelphia: 1829.

Hall, Francis. *Travels in Canada and the United States
in 1816 and 1817.* London: 1818.

Hamilton, Thomas. *Men and Manners in America.* Philadelphia: 1833.

Harris, William T. *Remarks made during a Tour through
the United States in 1817, 1818, and 1819.* 1821.

Hartwell, Henry. *The Present State of Virginia*. London: 1727.

Hinke, William J., ed. "Report of the Journey of Francis Louis Michel from Berne, Switzerland, to Virginia, October, 1701-December 1, 1702." *Virginia Magazine of History and Biography*, 24 (April, 1916).

Hodgson, Adam. *Letters from North America, Written during a Tour of the United States and Canada*. 2 vols. London: 1824.

Ingraham, Joseph Hold. *The South-West: By a Yankee*. New York: 1835.

Irving, John B. *A Day on Cooper River*. Charleston: 1842.

Johnston, Gideon. *Carolina Chronicle*. Berkeley: 1946.

Jones, Hugh. *The Present State of Virginia*. Chapel Hill: 1956.

Knight, Henry C. *Letters from the South and West*. Chapel Hill: 1824.

Latrobe, Charles J. *The Rambler in North America 1832-1833*. 2 vols. New York: 1835.

Lawson, John. *A New Voyage to Carolina*. Chapel Hill: 1967.

Lewis, George. *Impressions of America*. Edinburgh: 1845.

Lyell, Charles. *Travels in North America, Canada, and Nova Scotia*. 2 vols. London: 1845.

_____. *A Second Visit to the United States of North America*. 2 vols. New York: 1850.

Martineau, Harriet. *Society in America*. 3 vols. London: 1837.

_____. *Retrospect of Western Travel*. 3 vols. London: 1838.

Mead, Whitman. *Travels in North America*.

Moffatt, L. G. and J. M. Carriere, eds. "A Frenchman Visits Norfolk, Fredericksburg, and Orange County, 1816." *Virginia Magazine of History and Biography*, 53 (July, 1945).

Murat, Achille. *America and the Americans*. New York: 1849.

Nichols, Thomas Low. *Forty Years of American Life, 1821-1861*. New York: 1937.

O'Connor, John. *Wanderings of a Vagabond*. New York: 1873.

O'Ferrall, S. A. *A Ramble of Six Thousand Miles Through the United States of America*. London: 1832.

Olmstead, Frederick Law. *A Journey in the Back Country, 1853-1854*. New York: 1860.

_____. *A Journey in the Seaboard Slave States*. New York: 1856.

_____. *The Cotton Kingdom: A Traveller's Observations on Cotton and Slavery in the American Slave States, Based upon Three Volumes of Journeys and Investigations by the Same Author*. New York: 1853.

Palliser, John. *Solitary Rambles*. London: 1853.

Pearson, Elizabeth, ed. *Letters from Port Royal, 1862-1868*. New York: 1906.

Pollard, Edward. *Black Diamonds Gathered in the Darkey Homes of the South*. New York: 1859.

Power, Tyrone. *Impressions of America, During the Years 1833, 1834, and 1835*. London: 1836.

Pulszky, Francis and Theresa. *White, Red, and Black*. 3 vols. London: 1836.

Redpath, James. *The Roving Editor, Or, Talks with Slaves in the Southern States*. New York: 1859.

Rogers, George. *Memoranda of the Experience, Labors, and Travels of a Universalist Preacher*. Cincinatti: 1845.

Russell, William Howard. *My Diary North and South*. New York: 1862.

Sealsfield, Charles. *The Americans as They Are, Described in a Tour through the Valley of the Mississippi*. London: 1828.

Shelley, Fred, ed. "The Journal of Ebeneezer Hazard in Virginia, 1777." *Virginia Magazine of History and Biography*, 62 (October, 1954).

Stewart, Catherine. *New Homes in the West*. Nashville: 1843.

Stirling, James. *Letters from the Slave States*. London: 1857.

Stoddard, Amos. *Sketches, Historical and Descriptive of Louisiana*. Philadelphia: 1812.

Stuart-Wortley. *Travels in the United States, Etc., During 1849 and 1850*. 3 vols. London: 1851.

Sturge, Joseph. *A Visit to the United States of America in 1841*. London: 1842.

Sutcliff, Robert. *Travels in Some Parts of North America in the Years 1804, 1805 & 1806*. York, Eng.: 1811.

Tasistro, Louis F. *Random Shots and Southern Breezes*. New York: 1842.

Thomson, William. *A Tradesman's Travels*. Edinburgh: 1842.

Younger, Edward, ed. "A Yankee Reports on Virginia, 1842-1843: Letters from John Adam Kasson." *Virginia Magazine of History and Biography*, 56 (October, 1948).

WHITE REPORTS AND MEMOIRS

Abbey, Kathryn T., ed. "Documents Relating to El Destino and Chemonie Plantations, Middle Florida, 1828-1868." *Florida Historical Society Quarterly*, 7 (January, 1929).

Andrews, Garnett. *Reminiscences of an Old Georgia Lawyer*. Atlanta: 1870.

Avirett, James Battle. *The Old Plantation: How We Lived in Great House and Cabin before the War*. New York: 1901.

Bailey, Robert. *The Life and Adventures of Robert Bailey*. Richmond: 1822.

Banks, Mary Ross. *Bright Days in Old Plantation Home*. Boston: 1882.

Battle, Kemp P. *Memories of an Old-Time Tar Heel*. Chapel Hill: 1945.

Brackenridge, H. M. *Recollections of Persons and Places in the West*. Philadelphia: 1868.

Burke, Emily P. *Reminiscences of Georgia*. Oberlin: 1850.

Burwell, Letitia M. *Plantation Reminiscences*. Owensboro: 1878.

Candler, Myrtil Lon. "Reminiscences of Life in Georgia During the 1850s and 1860s." *Georgia Historical Quarterly*, 33 (June, 1949).

Chester, Samuel. *Pioneer Days in Arkansas*. Richmond: 1927.

Clayton, Victoria Virginia. *White and Black Under the Old Regime*. Milwaukee: 1899.

Clinkscales, John G. *On the Old Plantation: Reminiscences of His Childhood*. Spartanburg: 1916.

De Saussure, Nancy Bostick. *Old Plantation Days, Being Recollections of Southern Life before the Civil War*. New York: 1909.

Devereux, Margaret. *Plantation Sketches*. Cambridge: 1906.

"Diary of Col. William Bolling of Bolling Hall." *Virginia Magazine of History and Biography*, 43 (October, 1935).

Drake, Daniel. *Pioneer Life in Kentucky 1795-1800*. New York: 1948.

DuBose, John W. "Recollections of the Plantations." *Alabama Historical Quarterly*, 1 (Spring, 1930).

Duke, Basil W. *Reminiscences of General Basil W. Duke, CSA*. Garden City: 1911.

Easterby, J. H., ed. "Charles Cotesworth Pinckney's Plantation Diary, April 6-December 15, 1818." *South Carolina Historical and Genealogical Magazine*, 41 (October, 1940).

Etzenhouser, Elder R. *From Palmyra, N.Y., 1830, to Independence, Mo., 1894*. Independence: 1894.

Evans, Gladys C. and Theodora B. Marshall, eds. "Plantation Report From the Papers of Levin R. Marshall of 'Richmond,' Natchez, Mississippi." *Journal of Mississippi History*, 3 (January, 1941).

Felton, Rebecca Latimer. *Country Life in Georgia in the Days of My Youth*. Atlanta: 1919.

Fulkerson, H. S. *Random Recollections of Early Days in Mississippi*. Vicksburg: 1885.

Gilmer, George R. *Sketches of Some of the First Settlers of Upper Georgia, of the Cherokees, and the Author*. New York: 1855.

Green, Fletcher M., ed. *Ferry Hill Plantation Journal, January 4, 1838-January 15, 1839*. Chapel Hill: 1961.

Griffith, Lucille, ed. "The Plantation Record Book of Brookdale Farm, Amite County, 1856-1857." *Journal of Mississippi History*, 7 (January, 1945).

Hallum, John. *Diary of an Old Lawyer*. Nashville: 1895.

"Journal of Col. James Gordon." *William and Mary Quarterly*, 1st Series, 12 (July, 1903).

"Journal of John Barnwell." *Virginia Magazine of History and Biography*, 6 (July, 1898).

Joyce, John A. *A Checkered Life*. Chicago: 1883.

Kemble, Francis A. *Journal of a Residence on a Georgian Plantation in 1838-1839*. New York: 1863.

Le Conte, Joseph. *The Autobiography of Joseph Le Conte*. New York: 1903.

Macon, T. J. *Life's Gleanings*. Richmond: 1913.

Mallard, Robert Q. *Plantation Life Before Emancipation*. Richmond: 1892.

Maury, Dabney H. *Recollections of a Virginian*. New York: 1894.

Meek, A. B. *Romantic Passages in Southwestern History*. Mobile: 1857.

Michaux, R. R. *Sketches of Life in North Carolina*. Cutler: 1894.

Morton, Louis, ed. "The Daybook of Robert Wormeley Carter of Sabine Hall, 1766." *Virginia Magazine of History and Biography*, 68 (July, 1960).

Morton, Marmaduke B. *Kentuckians Are Different*. Louisville: 1938.

Paschal, George W. *Ninety-Four Years--Agnes Paschal*. Washington, D.C.: 1871.

Pendleton, James M. *Reminiscences of a Long Life*. Louisville: 1891.

Peterson, Walter F. "Slavery in the 1850s: The Recollections of an Alabama Unionist." *Alabama Historical Quarterly*, 39 (Fall and Winter, 1968).

Redd, John. "Reminiscences of Western Virginia, 1770-1790." *Virginia Magazine of History and Biography*, 6 (April, 1899).

Salley, A. S., ed. "Journal of General Peter Horry." *South Carolina Historical and Genealogical Magazine*, 39 (October, 1938); 40 (July, 1939); and 41 (January, 1940).

Shaler, Nathaniel Southgate. *Autobiography*. Boston: 1909.

Sims, J. Marion. *The Story of My Life*. New York: 1884.

Smedes, Susan Dabney. *Memorials of a Southern Planter*. Baltimore: 1887.

Stafford, G. M., ed. "The Autobiography of George Mason Graham." *Louisiana Historical Quarterly*, 20 (January, 1937).

Stoney, Samuel G., ed. "The Memoirs of Frederick Augustus Porcher." *South Carolina Historical and Genealogical Magazine*, 44 (July, 1943).

Swisshelm, Jane Grey. *Half a Century*. Chicago: 1880.

Torian, Sarah H., ed. "Ante-Bellum and War Memories of Mrs. Telfair Hodgson." *Georgia Historical Quarterly*, 27 (December, 1943).

Washington, Amanda. *How Beauty Was Saved*. New York: 1907.

Wilkinson, Eliza. *Letters of Eliza Wilkinson*. New York: 1839.

Wood, Norman B. *The White Side of a Black Subject*. Chicago: 1894.

Chapter 4
The Background of Slavery

GENERAL STUDIES

Albanese, Anthony. *The Plantation School*. New York: 1976.

Alexander, Herbert B. "Brazilian and United States Slavery Compared." *Journal of Negro History*, 7 (October, 1922).

Aptheker, Herbert. *Essays in the History of the American Negro: The Struggles of the Negro People for Emancipation During the Main Epochs of their Country's History*. New York: 1945.

Bain, Mildred and Ervin Lewis, eds. *From Freedom to Freedom. African Roots in American Soil*. New York: 1977.

Benners, Alfred H. *Slavery and Its Results*. Macon: 1923.

Bennett, Lerone Jr. *Before the Mayflower*. Chicago: 1969.

Berry, Mary Frances and John W. Blassingame. *Long Memory. The Black Experience in America*. New York: 1982.

Blassingame, John W. *The Slave Community: Plantation Life in the Antebellum South*. New York: 1972.

Brandfon, Robert. "Specific Purposes and the General Past: Slaves and Slavery." *Journal of Interdisciplinary History*, 3 (Autumn, 1972).

Brawley, Benjamin. *A Short History of the American Negro*. New York: 1939.

_____. *A Social History of the Negro*. New York: 1921.

Bullock, Henry Allen. *A History of Negro Education in the South: From 1619 to the Present*. Cambridge: 1967.

Conrad, Alfred H. and John R. Meyer. *The Economics of Slavery and Other Studies in Econometric History.* Chicago: 1964.

Coombs, Norman. *The Black Experience in America.* New York: 1972.

Craven, Wesley F. *The Southern Colonies in the Seventeenth Century, 1607-1689.* Baton Rouge: 1949.

_____. *White, Red, and Black: The Seventeenth Century Virginian.* Charlottesville: 1971.

Cummings, John. *The Negro Population, 1790-1915.* Washington, D.C.: 1918.

David, Paul, Herbert G. Gutman, Richard Sutch, Peter Temin, and Gavin Wright. *Reckoning With Slavery. A Critical Study in the Quantitative History of American Negro Slavery.* New York: 1976.

David, Paul A. and Peter Temin. "Slavery: The Progressive Institution?" *Journal of Economic History,* 34 (September, 1974).

Davis, David Brion. *The Problem of Slavery in the Age of Revolution: 1770-1823.* Ithaca: 1975.

_____. *The Problem of Slavery in Western Culture.* Ithaca: 1966.

Davis, T. R. "Negro Servitude in the United States." *Journal of Negro History,* 8 (July, 1923).

Degler, Carl N. *Neither Black Nor White: Slavery and Race Relations in Brazil and the United States.* New York: 1971.

_____. "Slavery and the Genesis of American Race Prejudice." *Comparative Studies in History and Society,* 11 (October, 1959).

Dowd, Jerome. *The Negro in American Life.* New York: 1926.

Drimmer, Melvin. "Neither Black Nor White: Carl Degler's Study of Slavery in Societies." *Phylon,* 40 (March, 1979).

DuBois, W. E. B. *Black Folk Then and Now: An Essay in the History and Sociology of the Negro Race.* New York: 1939.

_____. *The Gift of Black Folk: The Negroes in the Making of America.* New York: 1970.

_____. *The Negro.* New York: 1915.

Dunn, Richard S. "A Tale of Two Plantations: Slave Life at Mesopotamia in Jamaica and Mount Airy in Virginia, 1799 to 1828." *William and Mary Quarterly*, 34 (January, 1977).

Eder, Donald Gray. "Time Under the Cross: The Tannenbaum Thesis Reappraised." *Agricultural History*, 50 (October, 1976).

Elkins, Stanley B. *Slavery: A Problem in American Institutional and Intellectual Life*. Chicago: 1959.

Engerman, Stanley L. and Eugene D. Genovese, eds. *Race and Slavery in the Western Hemisphere: Quantitative History*. Princeton: 1975.

Eppes, Nicholas W. *The Negro of the Old South*. Chicago: 1925.

Eppse, Merl R. *The Negro, Too, In American History*. Chicago: 1939.

Fogel, Robert W. and Stanley L. Engerman. *Time on the Cross. The Economics of American Negro Slavery*. Boston: 1974.

Foner, Laura and Eugene D. Genovese, eds. *Slavery in the New World: A Reader in Comparative Slavery*. Englewood Cliffs: 1969.

Foner, Philip S. *History of Black Americans: From Africa to the Emergence of the Cotton Kingdom*. Westport: 1975.

Foster, William Z. *The Negro People in American History*. New York: 1954.

Franklin, John Hope. *From Slavery to Freedom. A History of Negro Americans*. New York: 1981.

_____. *Racial Equality in America*. Chicago: 1976.

Frazier, E. Franklin. *The Negro in the United States*. New York: 1949.

Geneovese, Eugene D. *Roll, Jordan, Roll: The World the Slaves Made*. New York: 1974.

_____. *The Political Economy of Slavery: Studies in the Economy of the Slave South*. New York: 1965.

_____. *The Slave Economies*. New York: 1973.

_____. *In Red and Black: Marxian Explorations in Southern and Afro-American History*. New York: 1968.

Genovese, Eugene D. and Elizabeth Fox-Genovese. "The Slave Economies in Political Perspective." *Journal of American History*, 66 (June, 1979).

Gilmore, Al-Tony. *Revisiting Blassingame's The Slave Community: The Scholars Respond.* Westport: 1978.

Goldin, Claudia D. *Urban Slavery in the South, 1820-1860: A Quantitative History.* Chicago: 1976.

Gutman, Herbert G. *The Black Family in Slavery and Freedom, 1750-1925.* New York: 1976.

Haley, James T. *Afro-American Encyclopedia.* New York: 1895.

Haynes, Robert V., ed. *Blacks in White America Before 1865.* New York: 1972.

Hart, Albert B. *Slavery and Abolition, 1831-1841.* New York: 1906.

Harding, Vincent. *There Is a River: The Black Struggle for Freedom in America.* New York: 1981.

Harlan, Louis R. *The Negro in American History.* Washington, D.C.: 1965.

Herskovits, Melville J. *The American Negro, A Study in Racial Crossing.* New York: 1928.

_____. *The Myth of the Negro Past.* Chicago: 1941.

Hine, William C. "American Slavery and Russian Serfdom: A Preliminary Comparison." *Phylon,* 36 (December, 1975).

Hoetnik, H. *Slavery and Race Relations in the Americas: Comparative Notes on Their Nature and Nexus.* New York: 1973.

Hofstadter, Richard. "U. B. Phillips and the Plantation Legend." *Journal of Negro History,* 29 (April, 1944).

Huggins, Nathan. *Black Odyssey: The Afro-American Ordeal in Slavery.* New York: 1977.

Jernegan, Marcus W. *Laboring and Dependent Classes in Colonial America, 1607-1783.* Chicago: 1931.

Johnson, Charles S. *The Negro in American Civilization.* New York: 1930.

Johnson, James Hugo. *Race Relations in Virginia and Miscegenation in the South: 1776-1860.* Amherst: 1970.

Jordan, Winthrop D. *White Over Black: American Attitudes Toward the Negro, 1550-1812.* Chapel Hill: 1968.

Klein, Herbert S. *Slavery in the Americas: A Comparative Study of Virginia and Cuba.* Chicago: 1967.

Lacy, Dan. *The White Use of Blacks in America.* New York: 1972.

Levine, Lawrence. *Black Culture and Black Consciousness. Afro-American Folk Thought From Slavery to Freedom.* New York: 1977.

Lincoln, C. Eric. *The Negro Pilgrimage in America.* New York: 1967.

Logan, Rayford W. *The Negro in the United States.* New York: 1957.

Low, W. Augustus and Virgil A. Cliff, eds. *Encyclopedia of Black America.* New York: 1981.

Luraghi, Raimondo. *The Rise and Fall of the Plantation South.* New York: 1978.

Lynd, Staughton. "Rethinking Slavery and Reconstruction." *Journal of Negro History,* 50 (July, 1965).

Mallard, Robert Q. *Plantation Life before Emancipation.* Richmond: 1892.

Mather, Frank L. *Who's Who of the Colored Race.* New York: 1915.

McPherson, James M. "Slavery and Race." *Perspectives in American History,* 3 (1969).

Meier, August and Elliott Rudwick. *Along the Color Line: Explorations in the Black Experience.* Urbana: 1976.

_____. *From Plantation to Ghetto: An Interpretive History of American Negroes.* New York: 1976.

_____. *The Making of Black America.* New York: 1969.

Morgan, Edmund. "Slavery and Freedom: The American Paradox." *Journal of American History,* 59 (June, 1979).

Mullin, Gerald W. "Rethinking American Negro Slavery from the Vantage Point of the Colonial Era." *Louisiana Studies,* 12 (Summer, 1973).

Myrdal, Gunner. *An American Dilemma: The Negro Problem and American Democracy.* New York: 1944.

Nash, Gary B. *Red, White, and Black: The Peoples of Early America.* Englewood Cliffs: 1974.

Nash, Gary B. and Richard Weiss. *The Great Fear: Race in the Mind of America.* New York: 1970.

Nearing, Scott. *Black America.* New York: 1929.

Ottley, Roi. *Black Odyssey: The Story of the Negro in America.* New York: 1948.

Owens, Leslie Howard. *This Species of Property: Slave Life and Culture in the Old South*. New York: 1976.

Pease, Jane H. and William H. Pease. *They Who Would Be Free: Blacks' Search for Freedom*. New York: 1974.

Phillips, Ulrich B. *American Negro Slavery*. New York: 1918.

_____. *Life and Labor in the Old South*. Boston: 1929.

Quarles, Benjamin. *The Negro in the Making of America*. New York: 1968.

Rawick, George. *From Sundown to Sunup. The Making of the Slave Community*. Westport: 1972.

Redding, J. Saunders. *The Lonesome Road*. Garden City: 1958.

_____. *They Came in Chains: Americans from Africa*. Philadelphia: 1950.

Rice, C. Duncan. *The Rise and Fall of Black Slavery*. Baton Rouge: 1976.

Richardson, Clement. *The National Cyclopedia of the Colored Race*. New York: 1919.

Rose, Peter I., ed. *Americans from Africa*. New York: 1970.

Rose, Willie Lee. *Slavery and Freedom*. New York: 1981.

Rubin, Vera, et al. *Plantation Systems of the New World*. Washington, D.C.: 1959.

Sowell, Thomas. *Race and Economics*. New York: 1975.

Stampp, Kenneth. *The Peculiar Institution. Slavery in the Antebellum South*. New York: 1956.

Szed, John F., ed. *Black America*. New York: 1970.

Takaki, Ronald T. *Iron Cages: Race and Culture in Nineteenth Century America*. New York: 1979.

Tannenbaum, Frank. *Slave and Citizen: The Negro in the Americas*. New York: 1947.

Thorpe, Earl E. *The Central Theme of Black History*. Durham: 1969.

Toppin, Edgar A. *Blacks in America*. New York: 1971.

Toplin, Robert Brent. "Reinterpreting Comparative Race Relations: The United States and Brazil." *Journal of Black Studies*, 2 (September, 1971).

Wade, Richard C. *Slavery in the Cities: The South, 1820-1860*. New York: 1964.

Washington, Booker T. *The Story of the Negro*. New York: 1909.

Wax, Darold D. "The Negro in Early America." *Social Studies*, 60 (March, 1969).

Weatherford, W. D. *The Negro from Africa to America*. New York: 1924.

Williams, Chancellor. *The Destruction of Black Civilization: Great Issues of a Race from 4500 B.C. to 2000 A.D.* Chicago: 1974.

Williams, George Washington. *A History of the Negro Race in America from 1619 to 1880*. New York: 1883.

Williams, Mary Wilhelmine. "The Treatment of Negro Slaves in the Brazilian Empire: A Comparison with the United States of America." *Journal of Negro History*, 15 (July, 1930).

Woodson, Carter G. *Education of the Negro Prior to 1861*. New York: 1915.

_____. *The Negro in Our History*. Washington, D.C.: 1927.

THE AFRICAN BACKGROUND

Adamu, Mahdi. *The Hausa Factor in West African History*. Zaria, Nigeria: 1978.

Ajayi, J. F. A. and Michael Crowder, eds. *History of West Africa*. 2 vols. New York: 1972 and 1974.

Akinjoghin, J. A. *Dahomey and Its Neighbors, 1708-1818*. Cambridge: 1967.

Argyle, W. J. *The Fon of Dahomey*. Oxford: 1966.

Archin, Kwame. "The Structure of Greater Ashanti." *Journal of African History*, 8 (No. 3, 1967).

Armattoe, R. E. G. *The Golden Age of West African Civilization*. Londonderry: 1946.

Bastide, Roger. *African Civilisations in the New World*. New York: 1971.

_____. *Drums and Shadows*. New York: 1972.

Bennett, Norman R. *Africa and Europe from Roman Times to the Present*. New York: 1975.

Birmingham, David. *The Portuguese Conquest of Angola*. London: 1965.

_____. *Trade and Conflict in Angola, 1483-1790*. Oxford: 1966.

Blake, John W. *European Beginnings in West Africa, 1454-1578*. London: 1937.

_____. *Europeans in West Africa, 1450-1560*. London: 1942.

Bovill, Edward W. *The Golden Trade of the Moors*. London: 1958.

Boxer, C. R. *The Dutch Seaborne Empire, 1600-1800*. London: 1965.

_____. *The Portuguese Seaborne Empire, 1415-1825*. London: 1969.

Burton, William F. P. *The Magic Drum*. New York: 1961.

Crosby, Alfred W. *The Columbian Exchange: Biological and Cultural Consequences of 1492*. Westport: 1972.

Curtin, Phillip D. *Economic Change in Precolonial Africa. Vol. 1: Senegambia in the Era of the Slave Trade*. Madison: 1975.

Davidson, Basil. *A History of West Africa to the Nineteenth Century*. New York: 1965.

_____. *The African Genius: An Introduction to African Social and Cultural History*. Boston: 1970.

_____. *The Lost Cities of Africa*. Boston: 1959.

Daaku, Y. D. *Trade and Politics on the Gold Coast, 1600-1720: A Study of the African Reaction to European Trade*. New York: 1970.

Debrunner, H. *Witchcraft in Ghana*. Kumasi: 1959.

Delafosse, Maurice. *The Negroes of Africa: History and Culture*. Washington, D.C.: 1931.

Dike, K. O. *Trade and Politics in the Niger Delta, 1830-1885*. London: 1956.

DuBois, W. E. B. *Black Folk: Then and Now*. New York: 1939.

_____. *The World and Africa*. New York: 1965.

Duffy, James. *Portuguese Africa*. Cambridge: 1959.

Egharenha, Jacob. *A Short History of Benin*. Ibadan: 1960.

Ellis, Alfred B. *The Tshi Speaking People of the Gold Coast*. London: 1887.

Ellis, George W. *Negro Culture in West Africa.* New York: 1914.

Evans, William McKee. "From the Land of Canaan to the Land of Guinea: The Strange Odyssey of the 'Sons of Ham'." *American Historical Review,* 85 (February, 1980).

Fage, J. D. *A History of West Africa.* London: 1969.

_____. *Ghana: A Historical Interpretation.* Madison: 1959.

_____. *Introduction to the History of West Africa.* Cambridge: 1959.

_____. "Slavery and the Slave trade in the Context of West African History." *Journal of African History,* 10 (No. 3, 1969).

_____. *States and Subjects in Sub-Sahara Africa.* Johannesburg: 1974.

Forde, C. Daryll, ed. *African Worlds: Studies in the Cosmological Ideas and Social Values of African Peoples.* London: 1954.

Forde, C. Daryll and G. I. Jones. *The Ibo and Ibibio-Speaking Peoples of South-Eastern Nigeria.* 1950.

Fynn, J. K. *Ashanti and Its Neighbors, 1700-1807.* London: 1971.

Grace, John. *Domestic Slaves in West Africa.* New York: 1975.

Grant, Douglas. *The Fortunate Slave.* New York: 1968.

Gray, Richard, ed. *The Cambridge History of Africa. Vol. 4: From c. 1600 to c. 1790.* New York: 1975.

Hallett, Robin. *Africa to 1875.* Ann Arbor: 1970.

Harris, Joseph E. *Africans and Their History.* New York: 1972.

Harms, Robert W. *River of Wealth, River of Sorrow. The Central Zaire Basin in the Era of the Slave and Ivory Trade, 1500 to 1891.* New Haven: 1981.

Herskovits, Melville J. *Dahomey, An Ancient West African Kingdom.* New York: 1938.

Hodgkin, Thomas, ed. *Nigerian Perspectives.* London: 1960.

Hopkins, A. G. *An Economic History of West Africa.* London: 1973.

Idowu, E. Bolaji. *Olodumare: God in Yoruba Belief.* London: 1962.

Johnson, Samuel. *The History of the Yorubas*. Evanston: 1964.

Johnson, H. A. S. *A Selection of Hausa Stories*. Oxford: 1966.

Josephy, Alvin M. Jr. *The Horizon History of Africa*. New York: 1971.

July, Robert. *Precolonial Africa: An Economic and Social History*. New York: 1975.

Junod, Henry P. and Alexandre A. Jacques. *The Wisdom of the Tonga-Shangaan People*. Pretoria: 1936.

Law, Robin. *The Oyo Empire, c. 1600-c. 1836: A West African Imperialism in the Era of the Atlantic Slave Trade*. Oxford: 1977.

Levtsion, Nehemia. *Muslims and Chiefs in West Africa: A Study of Islam in the Middle Volta Basin in the Pre-Colonial Period*. New York: 1969.

Little, Kenneth. *The Merde of Sierra Leone*. London: 1951.

Lovejoy, Paul E. "The Characteristics of Plantations in the Nineteenth-Century Sokoto Caliphate (Islamic West Africa)." *American Historical Review*, 84 (December, 1979).

Martin, Evelyn C. *The British West Africa Settlements, 1750-1821*. London: 1927.

Martin, Phyllis M. *The External Trade of the Loango Coast, 1576-1870: The Effects of Changing Commercial Relations on the Vili Kingdom of Loango*. New York: 1972.

Mbiti, John S. *New Testament Eschatology in an African Background*. New York: 1971.

_____. *The Prayers of African Religion*. Maryknoll: 1975.

McCall, Daniel F. and Norman R. Bennett, eds. *Aspects of West African Islam*. Boston: 1971.

Meek, Charles K. *The Northern Tribes of Nigeria*. 2 vols. London: 1925.

Miers, S. and I. Kopytoff, eds. *Slavery in Africa: Historical and Anthropological Perspectives*. Madison: 1977.

Mintz, S. W. "Toward an Afro-American History." *Journal of World History*, 13 (Summer, 1971).

Murdock, George P. *Africa: Its Peoples and Their Cultural History*. New York: 1959.

70

Newburry, C. W. *The Western Slave Coast and Its Rulers*.
     Oxford: 1961.

Niane, D. T. *Sundiata: An Epic of Old Mali*. Atlantic
     Highlands: 1965.

Northrup, David. *Trade Without Rulers: Pre-Colonial
     Economic Development in South-Eastern Nigeria*.
     Oxford: 1978.

O'Fahey, R. S. and J. L. Spaulding. *Kingdoms of the
     Sudan*. London: 1975.

Ojo, G. J. O. *Yoruba Culture: A Geographical Analysis*.
     London: 1966.

Oliver, Roland, ed. *The Cambridge History of Africa.
     Vol. 3: From c. 1050 to c. 1600*. New York: 1977.

Oliver, Roland and Anthony Atmore. *The African Middle
     Ages, 1400-1800*. New York: 1981.

Oliver, Roland and J. D. Fage. *A Short History of
     Africa*. Madison: 1959.

Parrinder, Geoffrey. *African Mythology*. London: 1967.

_____. *African Traditional Religion*. London: 1962.

Polanyi, Karl. *Dahomey and the Slave Trade*. Seattle:
     1966.

Priestley, Margaret. *West African Trade and Coast
     Society: A Family Study*. London: 1969.

Quinn, Charlotte A. *Mandingo Kingdoms of the Senegambia:
     Traditionalism, Islam, and European Expansion*.
     Evanston: 1972.

Rattray, Robert S. *The Ashanti*. Oxford: 1923.

_____. *Ashanti Law and Constitution*. Oxford: 1929.

Rodney, Walter. *A History of the Upper Guinea Coast,
     1545-1800*. Oxford: 1970.

_____. "Upper Guinea and the Significance of the
     Origins of Africans Enslaved in the New World."
     Journal of Negro History, 54 (October, 1969).

_____. *West Africa and the Atlantic Slave Trade*.
     Nairobi: 1967.

Roediger, David. "The Meaning of Africa for the Ameri-
     can Slave." *Journal of Ethnic Studies*, 4 (Winter,
     1977).

Ryder, A. F. *Benin and the Europeans, 1485-1897*.
     New York: 1969.

Samkange, Stanlake. *African Saga: A Brief Introduction to African History.* Nashville: 1971.

Skaggs, Merrill Maguire. "Roots: A New Black Myth." *Southern Quarterly,* 17 (Fall, 1978).

Skinner, Elliott P. *The Mossi of the Upper Volta.* Stanford: 1964.

Smith, Robert S. *Warfare and Diplomacy in Pre-Colonial West Africa.* London: 1976.

Talbot, Aamaury P. *Tribes of the Niger Delta.* London: 1932.

Thomas, Northcote. *Law and Customs of the Ibo.* London: 1914.

_____. *Law and Customs of the Timne and Other Tribes.* London: 1916.

Trimingham, J. Spencer. *A History of Islam in West Africa.* London: 1970.

Vogt, John. *Portuguese Rule on the Gold Coast, 1469-1682.* Athens: 1979.

Ward, W. E. F. *A History of the Gold Coast.* London: 1948.

Welch, Galbraith. *Africa Before They Came.* New York: 1965.

Williams, Wilson E. *Africa and the Rise of Capitalism.* Washington, D.C.: 1938.

Woodson, Carter G. *The African Background Outlined, or Handbook for the Study of the Negro.* Washington, D.C.: 1936.

THE SLAVE TRADE

Birmingham, David. *Trade and Conflict in Angola, 1483-1790.* Oxford: 1966.

Berlin, Ira. "The Slave Trade and the Development of Afro-American Society in English Mainland North America." *Southern Studies,* 20 (Summer, 1981).

Brady, Patrick S. "The Slave Trade and Sectionalism in South Carolina, 1787-1808." *Journal of Southern History,* 38 (November, 1972).

Cohn, Raymond L. and Richard A. Jensen. "Mortality Rates and the Slave Trader." *Essays in Economic and Business History,* (1981).

Coughtry, Jay. *The Notorious Triangle. Rhode Island and the Slave Trade, 1700-1807*. Philadelphia: 1981.

Curtin, Phillip D. *Economic Change in Precolonial Africa. Vol. 1: Senegambia in the Era of the Slave Trade*. Madison: 1975.

_____. "Epidemiology and the Slave Trade." *Political Science Quarterly*, 88 (June, 1968).

_____. *The Atlantic Slave Trade: A Census*. Madison: 1969.

Curtin, Phillip D. and Jan Vansina. "Sources of the Nineteenth Century Atlantic Slave Trade." *Journal of African History*, 5 (No. 2, 1964).

Curtin, Phillip D., Roger Anstey, and J. E. Inikori. "Discussion: Measuring the Atlantic Slave Trade." *Journal of African History*, 17 (No. 4, 1976).

Daaku, K. Y. *Trade and Politics on the Gold Coast, 1600-1720: A Study of the African Reaction to European Trade*. New York: 1970.

Davidson, Basil. *Black Mother: The Years of the African Slave Trade*. London: 1961.

_____. *The African Slave Trade: Pre-Colonial History, 1450-1850*. Boston: 1961.

Davies, Kenneth. *The Royal African Company*. London: 1957.

Dowd, Jerome. "The African Slave Trade." *Journal of Negro History*, 2 (January, 1917).

DuBois, W. E. B. *The Suppression of the African Slave Trade to the United States of America, 1638-1870*. New York: 1896.

Fage, J. D. "Slavery and the Slave Trade in the Context of West African History." *Journal of African History*, 10 (No. 3, 1969).

Foster, Herbert J. "Partners or Captives in Commerce? The Role of Africans in the Slave Trade." *Journal of Black Studies*, 6 (June, 1976).

Gemery, Henry A. and Jan S. Hogendorn, eds. *The Uncommon Market: Essays in the Economic History of the Atlantic Slave Trade*. New York: 1979.

Grace, John. *Domestic Slaves in West Africa*. New York: 1975.

Hendrix, James Paisley, Jr. "The Efforts to Reopen the African Slave Trade in Louisiana." *Louisiana Studies*, 10 (Spring, 1969).

High, James. "The African Gentleman, A Chapter in the Slave Trade." *Journal of Negro History*, 44 (July, 1959).

Kilson, Martin. "West African Societies and the Atlantic Slave Trade, 1441-1865." In Nathan I. Huggins, Martin Kilson, and Daniel M. Fox. *Key Issues in the Afro-American Experience*. Boston: 1971.

Klein, Herbert S. *The Middle Passage: Comparative Studies in the Atlantic Slave Trade*. Princeton: 1978.

Lachance, Paul F. "The Politics of Fear: French Louisianians and the Slave Trade, 1786-1809." *Plantation Society in the Americas*, 1 (June, 1979).

Law, Robin. *The Oyo Empire, c. 1600-c. 1836: A West African Imperialism in the Era of the Atlantic Slave Trade*. Oxford: 1977.

Littlefield, Daniel C. *Rice and Slaves. Ethnicity and the Slave Trade in Colonial South Carolina*. Baton Rouge: 1981.

Lydon, James G. "New York and the Slave Trade, 1700 to 1774." *William and Mary Quarterly*, 35 (April, 1978).

Mannix, Daniel and Malcolm Cowley. *Black Cargoes: A History of the Atlantic Slave Trade, 1518-1865*. New York: 1962.

Platt, Virginia Bever. "'And Don't Forget the Guinea Voyage': The Slave Trade of Aaron Lopez of Newport." *William and Mary Quarterly*, 32 (October, 1975).

Polanyi, Karl. *Dahomey and the Slave Trade*. Seattle: 1966.

Pope-Hennessy, James. *Sin of the Father: A Study of the Atlantic Slave Traders, 1441-1807*. 1968.

Rawley, James A. *The Transatlantic Slave Trade*. New York: 1981.

Rodney, Walter. *West Africa and the Atlantic Slave Trade*. Nairobi: 1967.

Stafford, Frances J. "Illegal Importations: Enforcement of the Slave Trade Laws Along the Florida Coast, 1810-1828." *Florida Historical Quarterly*, 46 (October, 1967).

Tansey, Richard. "Bernard Kendig and the New Orleans Slave Trade." *Louisiana History*, 23 (Spring, 1982).

Taylor, Joe G. "The Foreign Slave Trade in Louisiana after 1808." *Louisiana History*, 2 (Winter, 1960).

Verger, Pierre. *Bahia and the West African Trade, 1549-1851*. Ibadan: 1964.

Wax, Darold. "'A People of Beastly Living': Europe, Africa, and the Atlantic Slave Trade." *Phylon*, 41 (March, 1980).

_____. "Black Immigrants: The Slave Trade in Colonial Maryland." *Maryland Historical Magazine*, 73 (Spring, 1978).

_____. "Negro Imports into Pennsylvania, 1720-1766." *Pennsylvania History*, 32 (July, 1965).

_____. "Negro Resistance to the Early American Slave Trade." *Journal of Negro History*, 50 (January, 1966).

_____. "Quaker Merchants and the Slave Trade in Colonial Pennsylvania." *Pennsylvania Magazine of History and Biography*, 86 (April, 1962).

Wells, Tom Henderson. *The Slave Ship Wanderer*. Athens: 1967.

Williams, Eric. *Capitalism and Slavery*. Chapel Hill: 1944.

Wish, Harvey. "The Revival of the African Slave Trade in the United States, 1856-1860." *Mississippi Valley Historical Review*, 27 (March, 1941).

Wyndham, H. A. *The Atlantic and Slavery*. New York: 1935.

Chapter 5
The Institutions of Slavery

STATE AND REGIONAL STUDIES

Abel, Annie Heloise. *The Slaveholding Indians. Vol. 1: As Slaveholder and Secessionist.* Cleveland: 1915.

Allain, Mathe. "Slave Policies in French Louisiana." *Louisiana History*, 21 (Spring, 1980).

Ballagh, James C. *A History of Slavery in Virginia.* Baltimore: 1902.

Barr, Allwyn. *Black Texans: A History of Negroes in Texas, 1528-1971.* Austin: 1971.

Bassett, John Spencer. *Slavery and Servitude in the Colony of North Carolina.* Baltimore: 1896.

_____. *Slavery in the State of North Carolina.* Baltimore: 1899.

Beasley, Delilah. "Slavery in California." *Journal of Negro History*, 3 (January, 1918).

Billington, Monroe. "Black Slavery in Indian Territory: The Ex-Slave Narratives." *Chronicles of Oklahoma*, 60 (Spring, 1980).

Birnie, C. W. "The Education of the Negro in Charleston, South Carolina, before the Civil War." *Journal of Negro History*, 12 (January, 1927).

Brackett, Jeffrey R. *The Negro in Maryland. A Study of the Institution of Slavery.* Baltimore: 1889.

Brigham, R. I. "Negro Education in Antebellum Missouri." *Journal of Negro History*, 30 (October, 1945).

Channing, Edward. *The Narragansett Planters.* Baltimore: 1886.

Coleman, J. Winston, Jr. *Slavery Times in Old Kentucky.* Chapel Hill: 1940.

Colley, Henry S. *A Study of Slavery in New Jersey.* Baltimore: 1986.

Coulter, E. Merton. "A Century of a Georgia Plantation." *Mississippi Valley Historical Review*, 16 (December, 1929).

Craven, Wesley Frank. *Red, White, and Black: The Seventeenth Century Virginian*. Charlottesville: 1971.

Crockett, Norman L. *The Black Towns*. Lawrence: 1979.

Davis, Charles S. *The Cotton Kingdom in Alabama*. Montgomery: 1939.

Davis, E. A., ed. *Plantation Life in the Florida Parishes of Louisiana*. 1942.

Dethloff, Henry C. and Robert R. Jones. "Race Relations in Louisiana." *Louisiana History*, 10 (Fall, 1968).

Dick, Everett. *The Dixie Frontier: A Social History of the Southern Frontier from the First Transmontane Beginnings to the Civil War*. New York: 1964.

Duncan, John D. "Slavery Emancipation in Colonial South Carolina." *American Chronicle*, 1 (January, 1972).

Flanders, Ralph Betts. *Plantation Slavery in Georgia*. Chapel Hill: 1933.

Franklin, John Hope. "Slaves Virtually Free in Antebellum North Carolina." *Journal of Negro History*, 28 (July, 1943).

_____. "The Enslavement of Free Negroes in North Carolina." *Journal of Negro History*, 29 (October, 1944).

Greene, Lorenzo J. *The Negro in Colonial New England, 1620-1776*. New York: 1942.

_____. "The New England Negro as Seen in Advertisements for Runaway Slaves." *Journal of Negro History*, 29 (April, 1944).

Hamer, Marguerite B. "A Century before Manumission—Sidelights on Slavery in Mid-Eighteenth Century South Carolina." *North Carolina Historical Review*, 17 (July, 1940).

Herndon, G. Melvin. "Slavery in Antebellum Virginia: William Galt, Jr., 1839-1851, A Case Study." *Southern Studies*, 16 (Fall, 1977).

Hirsch, Leo H., Jr. "New York and the Negro, from 1783 to 1865." *Journal of Negro History*, 16 (October, 1931).

Hoffman, Edwin D. "From Slavery to Self-Reliance: The Record of Achievement of the Freedmen of the Sea Island Region." *Journal of Negro History*, 41 (January, 1956).

Jeltz, Wyatt F. "The Relations of Negroes and Choctaw and Chickasaw Indians." *Journal of Negro History*, 33 (January, 1948).

Johnson, Guion C. *Ante-Bellum North Carolina. A Social History*. Chapel Hill: 1937.

Johnson, Whittington B. "The Origin and Nature of African Slavery in Seventeenth Century Maryland." *Maryland Historical Magazine*, 73 (September, 1978).

Johnston, James Hugo. *Race Relations in Virginia and Miscegenation in the South, 1776-1860*. Amherst: 1970.

Johnston, William. *Slavery in Rhode Island, 1755-1776*. Providence: 1894.

Jordan, Weymouth T. *Ante-Bellum Alabama: Town and Country*. Tallahassee: 1957.

Jordan, Winthrop. "The Influence of the West Indies on New England Slavery." *William and Mary Quarterly*, 18 (April, 1961).

Katz, William Loren. *The Black West*. New York: 1971.

Klein, Herbert S. "Slaves and Shipping in Eighteenth Century Virginia." *Journal of Interdisciplinary History*, 5 (Winter, 1975).

Klingberg, Frank J. *An Appraisal of the Negro in Colonial South Carolina*. Washington, D.C.: 1941.

Lamon, Lester C. *Blacks in Tennessee, 1791-1970*. Knoxville: 1981.

Lapp, Rudolph M. *Blacks in Gold Rush California*. New Haven: 1977.

Littlefield, Daniel F. *Africans and Seminoles: From Removal to Emancipation*. Westport: 1977.

Lythgoe, Dennis L. "Negro Slavery in Utah." *Utah Historical Quarterly*, 39 (Winter, 1971).

Mabee, Carleton. *Black Education in New York State: From Colonial to Modern Times*. Syracuse: 1979.

McColley, Robert. *Slavery and Jeffersonian Virginia*. Urbana: 1964.

McDougle, Ivan. "Slavery in Kentucky." *Journal of Negro History*, 3 (July, 1918).

_____. *Slavery in Kentucky, 1792-1865.* Westport: 1970.

McGrady, Edward. *The History of South Carolina under Proprietary Government, 1670-1719.* New York: 1897.

McKee, Samuel. *Labor in Colonial New York, 1664-1776.* New York: 1935.

McManus, Edgar J. *A History of Negro Slavery in New York.* Syracuse: 1966.

_____. *Black Bondage in the North.* Syracuse: 1973.

Miller, M. Sammy. "The Negro in Delaware, 1638-1860." *Negro History Bulletin,* 36 (March, 1973).

Moody, V. Alton. "Slavery on Louisiana Sugar Plantations." *Louisiana Historical Quarterly,* 7 (Winter, 1924).

Mooney, Chase C. *Slavery in Tennessee.* Bloomington: 1957.

Moore, John Hebron. *Agriculture in Ante-Bellum Mississippi.* New York: 1958.

Moore, George. *A Note on Slavery in Massachusetts.* New York: 1866.

Morgan, Edmund. *American Slavery, American Freedom: The Ordeal of Colonial Virginia.* New York: 1975.

Morgan, Edwin. *Slavery in New York.* Washington, D.C.: 1891.

Moss, Simeon F. "The Persistence of Slavery and Involuntary Servitude in a Free State (1685-1866)." *Journal of Negro History,* 35 (July, 1950).

Mullin, Gerald W. *Flight & Rebellion: Slave Resistance in Eighteenth-Century Virginia.* New York: 1972.

Padgett, James A. "The Status of Slaves in Colonial North Carolina." *Journal of Negro History,* 14 (July, 1929).

Patrick, Elizabeth Nelson. "The Black Experience in Southern Nevada." *Nevada Historical Society Quarterly,* 22 (Fall, 1979).

Patterson, Caleb Perry. *The Negro in Tennessee, 1790-1865.* New York: 1968.

Porter, Kenneth W. "Florida Slaves and Free Negroes in the Seminole War, 1835-1842." *Journal of Negro History,* 28 (October, 1943).

_____. "Negroes and Indians on the Texas Frontier, 1831-1876." *Journal of Negro History*, 41 (July and October, 1956).

_____. "Negroes on the Southern Frontier, 1670-1753." *Journal of Negro History*, 33 (January, 1948).

_____. "Relations between Negroes and Indians within the Present Limits of the United States." *Journal of Negro History*, 17 (July, 1932).

_____. *The Negro on the American Frontier.* New York: 1971.

Prichard, Walter. "Routine on a Louisiana Sugar Plantation Under the Slavery Regime." *Mississippi Valley Historical Review*, 14 (September, 1927).

Rankin, David C. "The Tannenbaum Thesis Reconsidered: Slavery and Race Relations in Antebellum Louisiana." *Southern Studies*, 18 (Spring, 1979).

Riddell, William R. "The Slave in Early New York." *Journal of Negro History*, 13 (January, 1928).

Riley, Carroll L. "Blacks in the Early Southwest." *Ethnohistory*, 19 (Summer, 1972).

Robert, Joseph Clark. *The Tobacco Kingdom.* Durham: 1938.

Savage, W. Sherman. "The Negro in the History of the Pacific Northwest." *Journal of Negro History*, 13 (July, 1928).

_____. *Blacks in the West.* Westport: 1976.

Shugg, Roger W. *Origins of Class Struggle in Louisiana.* University, La.: 1939.

Sellers, James Benson. *Slavery in Alabama.* University, Ala.: 1950.

Sitterson, J. Carlyle. *Sugar Country: The Cane Sugar Industry in the South, 1753-1950.* Lexington: 1953.

Smith, Julia Floyd. *Slavery and Plantation Growth in Antebellum Florida, 1821-1860.* Gainesville: 1973.

Southall, Eugene P. "Negroes in Florida Prior to the Civil War." *Journal of Negro History*, 19 (January, 1934).

Stark, Bruce. "Slavery in Connecticut: A Re-Examination." *Connecticut Review*, 9 (November, 1975).

Steiner, Bernard C. *A History of Slavery in Connecticut.* Baltimore: 1893.

Strickland, Arvarh E. "Aspects of Slavery in Missouri, 1821." *Missouri Historical Review,* 65 (July, 1971).

Sunseri, Alvin R. "A Note on Slavery and the Black Man in New Mexico, 1846-1861." *Negro History Bulletin,* 38 (August/September, 1975).

Sydnor, Charles S. *Slavery in Mississippi.* New York: 1933.

Taylor, Joe Gray. *Negro Slavery in Louisiana.* Baton Rouge: 1963.

Taylor, Orville W. *Negro Slavery in Arkansas.* Durham: 1958.

Taylor, Quintard. "Slaves and Free Men: Blacks in the Oregon Country, 1840-1860." *Oregon Historical Quarterly,* 83 (Summer, 1982).

Taylor, Rosser Howard. *Slaveholding in North Carolina: An Economic View.* Chapel Hill: 1926.

Thornbrough, Emma Lou. *The Negro in Indiana: A Study of a Minority.* Indianapolis: 1957.

Thurman, A. Odell. "The Negro in California Before 1890." *Pacific Historian,* 20 (Spring, 1976).

Trexler, Harrison A. *Slavery in Missouri, 1804-1865.* Baltimore: 1914.

Turner, Edward R. *The Negro in Pennsylvania.* Washington, D.C.: 1911.

Turner, Wallace B. "Kentucky Slavery in the Last Ante-Bellum Decade." *Register of the Kentucky Historical Society,* (October, 1960).

Twombly, Robert C. and Robert H. Moore. "Black Puritan: The Negro in Seventeenth Century Massachusetts." *William and Mary Quarterly,* 24 (April, 1967).

Wax, Darold D. "Georgia and the Negro Before the American Revolution." *Georgia Historical Quarterly,* 51 (March, 1967).

Weatherby, William T. and Roi Ottey. *The Negro in New York: An Informal Social History.* New York: 1967.

Williams, Edwin L. "Negro Slavery in Florida." *Florida Historical Quarterly,* 27 (October, 1949) and 28 (January, 1950).

Wood, Peter H. *Black Majority: Negroes in Colonial South Carolina, From 1670 through the Stono Rebellion*. New York: 1974.

Wright, Marain T. *Education of Negroes in New Jersey*. New York: 1941.

LOCAL STUDIES

Africa, Philip. "Slaveholding in the Salem Community, 1771-1851." *North Carolina Historical Review*, 54 (July, 1977).

Beasley, Jonathan. "Blacks--Slave and Free--Vicksburg, 1850-1860." *Journal of Mississippi History*, 38 (February, 1976).

Camerota, Michael. "Westfield's Black Community, 1755-1905." *Historical Journal of Western Massachusetts*, 5 (Spring, 1976).

Campbell, Randolph. "Human Property: The Negro Slave in Harrison County, Texas, 1850-1860." *Southwestern Historical Quarterly*, 76 (April, 1973).

Corlew, Robert E. "Some Aspects of Slavery in Dickson County." *Tennessee Historical Quarterly*, 10 (September, 1931).

Coulter, C. Merton. "Slavery and Freedom in Athens, Georgia, 1860-1866." *Georgia Historical Quarterly*, 49 (September, 1965).

Davis, Russell H. *Black Americans in Cleveland from George Peake to Carl B. Stokes, 1796-1969*. Washington, D.C.: 1972.

Fischer, Roger A. "Racial Segregation in Ante-Bellum New Orleans." *American Historical Review*, 74 (February, 1969).

Flanders, Ralph Betts. "Two Plantations and a County of Antebellum Georgia." *Georgia Historical Quarterly*, 12 (March, 1928).

Gardner, Bettye. "Antebellum Black Education in Baltimore." *Maryland Historical Magazine*, 64 (Fall, 1969).

Garonzik, Joseph. "The Racial and Ethnic Make-up of Baltimore Neighborhoods, 1850-1870." *Maryland Historical Magazine*, 71 (Fall, 1976).

Geist, Christopher D. "Slavery Among the Indians: An Overview." *Negro History Bulletin*, 38 (August/September, 1975).

83

Goodstein, Anita S. "Black History on the Nashville Frontier, 1780-1810." *Tennessee Historical Quarterly*, 38 (Winter, 1979).

Halliburton, Janet. "Black Slavery in the Creek Nation." *Chronicles of Oklahoma*, 56 (Fall, 1978).

Halliburton, R., Jr. *Red Over Black: Black Slavery among the Cherokee Indians*. Westport: 1977.

Hoffecker, Carol E. "The Politics of Exclusion: Blacks in Nineteenth Century Wilmington, Delaware." *Delaware History*, 16 (April, 1974).

Hughes, John Starrett. "Lafayette County and the Aftermath of Slavery, 1861-1870." *Missouri Historical Review*, 75 (October, 1980).

Hunter, Lloyd A. "Slavery in St. Louis, 1804-1860." *Bulletin of the Missouri Historical Society*, 30 (July, 1974).

Ireland, Ralph R. "Slavery on Long Island: A Study of Economic Motivation." *Journal of Long Island History*, 2 (Spring, 1966).

Johnson, Kenneth R. "Slavery and Racism in Florence, Alabama, 1841-1862." *Civil War History*, 27 (June, 1981).

Katzman, David M. *Before the Ghetto: Black Detroit in the Nineteenth Century*. Urbana: 1973.

Miller, M. Sammy. "Slavery in an Urban Area--District of Columbia." *Negro History Bulletin*, 37 (August/September, 1974).

Mills, Gary B. *The Forgotten People. Cane River's Creoles of Color*. Baton Rouge: 1977.

Mohr, Clarence L. "Slavery in Oglethorpe County, Georgia, 1773-1865." *Phylon*, 33 (Spring, 1972.

Nash, Gary B. "Slaves and Slaveowners in Colonial Philadelphia." *William and Mary Quarterly*, 30 (April, 1973).

Nordstrom, Carl. "Slavery in a New York County: Rockland County, 1768-1827." *Afro-Americans in New York Life and History*, 1 (July, 1977).

Ohline, Howard A. "Georgetown, South Carolina: Racial Anxieties and Militant Behavior, 1802." *South Carolina Historical Magazine*, 53 (June, 1972).

Otto, John Solomon. "Slavery in a Coastal Community--Glynn County, 1790-1860." *Georgia Historical Quarterly*, 64 (Winter, 1979).

_____. "Slavery in the Mountains: Uell County,
Arkansas, 1840-1860." *Arkansas Historical Quarterly*, 39 (Spring, 1980).

_____. "The Case for Folk History: Slavery in the
Highlands South." *Southern Studies*, 20 (Summer,
1981).

Phifer, Edward W. "Slavery in Microcosm: Burke County,
North Carolina." *Journal of Southern History*, 28
(May, 1962).

Price, John Milton. "Slavery in Winn Parish."
Louisiana History, 8 (Spring, 1967).

Proctor, William G., Jr. "Slavery in Southwest Georgia." *Georgia Historical Quarterly*, 50 (March,
1965).

Reinders, Robert C. "Slavery in New Orleans in the
Decade before the Civil War." *Mid-America*, 44
(October, 1962).

Richter, William L. "Slavery in Baton Rouge, 1820-1860."
Louisiana History, 10 (Spring, 1969).

Rivers, Larry E. "Slavery in Microcosm: Leon County,
Florida, 1824-1860." *Journal of Negro History*,
46 (Fall, 1981).

Scarpino, Philip V. "Slavery in Callaway County,
Missouri: 1845-1855." *Missouri Historical Review*,
71 (October, 1976) and (April, 1977).

Scheiner, Seth M. *Negro Mecca: The Story of the Negro
in New York City*. New York: 1965.

Seip, Terry L. "Slaves and Free Negroes in Alexandria,
1850-1860." *Louisiana History*, 10 (Spring, 1969).

Smith, C. Calvin. "The Oppressed Oppressors: Negro
Slavery Among the Choctaw Indians of Oklahoma."
Red River Valley Historical Review, 2 (Summer, 1975).

Tate, Thad W. *The Negro in Eighteenth Century Williamsburg*. Williamsburg: 1965.

Tully, "Patterns of Slaveholding in Colonial Pennsylvania: Chester and Lancaster Counties, 1729-1758."
Journal of Social History, 6 (Spring, 1973).

Wade, Richard C. "The Negro in Cincinatti, 1800-1830."
Journal of Negro History, 39 (January, 1941).

Warner, Robert Austin. *New Haven Negroes: A Social
History*. New Haven: 1940.

Anderson, Ralph V. and Robert E. Gallman. "Slaves or Fixed Capital: Slave Labor and Southern Economic Development." *Journal of American History*, 64 (June, 1977).

Armstrong, Thomas F. "From Task Labor to Free Labor: The Transition along Georgia's Rice Coast, 1820-1880." *Georgia Historical Quarterly*, 64 (Winter, 1980).

Aufhauser, R. Keith. "Slavery and Scientific Management." *Journal of Economic History*, 33 (December, 1973).

_____. "Slavery and Technological Change." *Journal of Economic History*, 34 (March, 1974).

Campbell, Randolph. "The Productivity of Slave Labor in East Texas: A Research Note." *Louisiana Studies*, 13 (Summer, 1974).

Canarella, Giorgio and John A. Tomaske. "The Optimal Utilization of Slaves." *Journal of Economic History*, 35 (September, 1975).

Cunliffe, Marcus. *Chattel Slavery and Wage Slavery: The Anglo-American Context, 1830-1860*. Athens: 1979.

David, Paul A. and Peter Temin. "Capitalist Masters, Bourgeois Slaves." *Journal of Interdisciplinary History*, 5 (Winter, 1975).

Della M., Jr. "The Problems of Negro Labor in the 1850s." *Maryland Historical Magazine*, 66 (Spring, 1971).

Dew, Charles B. "Black Ironworkers and the Slave Insurrection Panic of 1856." *Journal of Southern History*, 41 (August, 1975).

_____. "David Ross and the Oxford Iron Works: A Study of Industrial Slavery in the Early Nineteenth-Century South." *William and Mary Quarterly*, 31 (April, 1974).

_____. "Disciplining Slave Ironworkers in the Antebellum South: Coercion, Conciliation, and Accomodation." *American Historical Review*, 79 (April, 1974).

Eaton, Clement. "Slave-Hiring in the Upper South: A Step Toward Freedom." *Mississippi Valley Historical Review*, 46 (March, 1960).

Findlay, Ronald. "Slavery, Incentives, and Manumission: A Theoretical Model." *Journal of Political Economy*, 83 (October, 1975).

Foner, Philip S. and Ronald L. Lewis. *The Black Worker to 1869*. Philadelphia: 1978.

Foner, Philip S. *Organized Labor and the Black Worker, 1619-1973*. New York: 1974.

Green, Barbara L. "Slave Labor at the Maramec Iron Works, 1828-1850." *Missouri Historical Review*, 73 (January, 1979).

Handlin, Oscar and Mary Handlin. "Origins of the Southern Labor System." *William and Mary Quarterly*, 7 (April, 1950).

Harper, C. W. "House Servants and Field Hands: Fragmentation in the Antebellum Slave Community." *North Carolina Historical Review*, 55 (January, 1978).

Harris, Robert L., Jr. "The Race Driver: His Role in Slave Management." *South Carolina Historical Magazine*, 82 (October, 1981).

Haywood, C. Robert. "Mercantilism and Colonial Slave Labor, 1700-1763." *Journal of Southern History*, 23 (November, 1957).

Hughes, Sarah S. "Slaves for Hire: The Allocation of Black Labor in Elizabeth City County, Virginia, 1872-1810." *William and Mary Quarterly*, 35 (April, 1978).

Jernegan, Marcus W. "Slavery and the Beginnings of Industrialism in America." *American Historical Review*, 25 (January, 1920).

Lander, Ernest M., Jr. "Slave Labor in South Carolina Cotton Mills." *Journal of Negro History*, 38 (April, 1953).

Lewis, Ronald L. *Coal, Iron, and Slaves: Industrial Slavery in Maryland and Virginia, 1715-1865*. Westport: 1979.

Luraghi, Raimondo. "Wage Labor in the 'Rice Belt' of Northern Italy and Slave Labor in the American South--A First Approach." *Southern Studies*, 9 (Summer, 1971).

Menard, Russell. "From Servants to Slaves: The Transformation of the Chesapeake Labor System." *Southern Studies*, 16 (Winter, 1977).

Messner, William F. *Freedmen and the Ideology of Free Labor: Louisiana, 1862-1865*. Lafayette: 1978.

Morris, Richard B. "The Measure of Bondage in the Slave States." *Mississippi Valley Historical Review*, 41 (September, 1954).

Newton, James E. and Ronald Lewis, eds. *The Other Slaves: Mechanics, Artisans, and Craftsmen.* Boston: 1978.

Phillips, Ulrich B. "Plantations with Slave and Free Labor." *American Historical Review*, 30 (July, 1925).

Preyer, Norris W. "The Historian, the Slave, and the Antebellum Textile Industry." *Journal of Negro History*, 46 (April, 1961).

Scarborough, William Dauffman. *The Overseer: Plantation Management in the Old South.* Baton Rouge: 1966.

Starobin, Robert S. *Industrial Slavery in the Old South.* New York: 1970.

Stealey, John Edmund, III. "The Responsibilities and Liabilities of the Bailee of Slave Labor in Virginia." *American Journal of Legal History*, 12 (October, 1968).

Taylor, Paul S. "Plantation Laborers before the Civil War." *Agricultural History*, 28 (January, 1954).

Usner, Daniel H., Jr. "From African Captivity to American Slavery: The Introduction of Black Laborers to Colonial Louisiana." *Louisiana History*, 20 (Winter, 1979).

Van Deburg, William L. *The Slave Drivers: Black Agricultural Supervisors in the Antebellum South.* Westport: 1979.

Wax, Darold D. "The Demand for Slave Labor in Colonial Pennsylvania." *Pennsylvania History*, 34 (October, 1967).

Wesley, Charles H. *Negro Labor in the United States, 1850-1925: A Study in American Economic History.* New York: 1927.

Woolfolk, George R. "Cotton Capitalism and Slave Labor in Texas." *Southwestern Social Science Quarterly*, 22 (June, 1956).

SLAVE CONTROL

Alpert, Jonathan L. "The Origin of Slavery in the United States--The Maryland Precedent." *American Journal of Legal History*, 14 (July, 1970).

Bardolph, Richard, ed. *The Civil Rights Record: Black Americans and the Law, 1849-1970.* New York: 1970.

Betty-Brown, Florence R. "Legal Status of Arkansas Negroes Before Emancipation." *Arkansas Historical Quarterly,* 28 (Spring, 1969).

Billings, Warren N. "The Cases of Fernando and Elizabeth Key: A Note on the Status of Blacks in Seventeenth-Century Virginia." *William and Mary Quarterly,* 30 (July, 1973).

Boles, John B. "Tension in a Slave Society: The Trial of Reverend Jacob Gruber." *Southern Studies,* 18 (Summer, 1979).

Brasseaux, Carl A. "The Administration of Slave Regulations in French Louisiana." *Louisiana History,* 21 (Spring, 1980).

Brewer, James H. "Legislation Designed to Control Slavery in Wilmington and Fayetteville." *North Carolina Historical Review,* 30 (April, 1953).

Calligaro, Lee. "The Negro's Legal Status in Pre-Civil War New Jersey." *New Jersey History,* 85 (Fall-Winter, 1967).

Catterall, Helen Tannicliff. *Judicial Cases Concerning American Slavery and the Negro.* 5 vols. Washington, D.C.: 1926-1937.

Clark, Ernest James, Jr. "Aspects of the North Carolina Slave Code, 1715-1860." *North Carolina Historical Review,* 39 (Spring, 1962).

Crawford, Paul. "A Footnote on Courts for Trial of Negroes in Colonial Pennsylvania." *Journal of Black Studies,* 5 (September, 1974).

Dew, Charles B. "Disciplining Slave Ironworkers in the Antebellum South: Coercion, Conciliation, and Accomodation." *American Historical Review,* 79 (April, 1974).

Edwards, John C. "Slave Justice in Four Middle Georgia Counties." *Georgia Historical Quarterly,* 57 (Summer, 1973).

Engerman, Stanley, "Some Considerations Relating to Property Rights in Man." *Journal of Economic History,* 33 (March, 1973).

Forness, Norman O. "The Master, the Slave, and the Patent Laws: A Vignette of the 1850s." *Prologue,* 12 (Spring, 1980).

Gara, Larry. "The Fugitive Slave Law: A Double Para-
     dox." *Civil War History*, 10 (September,
     1964).

Hall, Gwendolyn M. *Social Control in Slave Plantation
     Societies*. Boston: 1971.

Halliburton, R. "Black Slave Control in the Cherokee
     Nation." *Journal of Ethnic Studies*, 3 (Summer,
     1975).

Handlin, Oscar and Mary Handlin. "The Origins of Negro
     Slavery." In *Race and Nationality in American
     Life*. New York: 1957.

Hast, Adele. "The Legal Status of the Negro in Virgin-
     ia, 1705-1765." *Journal of Negro History*, 54
     (July, 1969).

Higginbothan, A. Leon, Jr. "Racism and the Early Amer-
     ican Legal Process, 1619-1896." *Annals of the
     American Academy of Political and Social Science*,
     407 (May, 1973).

Henry, Howell M. *Police Control of the Slave in South
     Carolina*. Emery: 1914.

Hindus, Michael S. "Black Justice under White Law:
     Criminal Prosecution of Blacks in Antebellum South
     Carolina." *Journal of American History*, 63
     (September, 1976).

Howard, Warren S. *American Slavers and the Federal
     Law, 1837-1862*. Berkeley: 1963.

Imes, William Lloyd. "The Legal Status of Free Negroes
     and Slaves in Tennessee." *Journal of Negro History*,
     4 (July, 1919).

Jordan, Winthrop D. "American Chiaroscuro: The Status
     and Definition of Mulattoes in the British Colon-
     ies." *William and Mary Quarterly*, 19 (April,
     1962).

Lack, Paul D. "Slavery and Vigilantism in Austin,
     Texas, 1840-1860." *Southwestern Historical Quart-
     erly*, 85 (July, 1981).

Mangum, Charles S. *The Legal Status of the Negro*.
     Chapel Hill: 1940.

McPherson, Robert G. "Georgia Slave Trials, 1837-1849."
     American Journal of Legal History, 4 (July, 1960).

Mecklin, John M. "The Evolution of the Slave Status in
     American Democracy." *Journal of Negro History*,
     2 (April and July, 1917).

Moore, Wilbert E. "Slave Law and the Social Structure."
Journal of Negro History, 26 (January, 1941).

Nash, A. E. Keir. "The Texas Supreme Court and Trial
Rights of Blacks, 1845-1860." *Journal of American
History*, 58 (December, 1971).

Nordstrom, Carl. "The New York Slave Code." *Afro-
Americans in New York Life and Thought*, 4 (January,
1980).

Olson, Edwin. "The Slave Code in Colonial New York."
Journal of Negro History, 29 (April, 1944).

Palmer, Paul C. "Servant into Slave: The Evolution of
the Legal Status of the Negro Laborer in Colonial
Virginia." *South Atlantic Quarterly*, 65 (Summer,
1966).

Richardson, Joe M. "Florida Black Codes." *Florida
Historical Quarterly*, 47 (April, 1969).

Shofner, Jerrell H. "Custom, Law, and History: The
Enduring Influence of Florida's 'Black Code'."
Florida Historical Quarterly, 55 (January, 1976).

Sirmans, M. Eugene. "The Legal Status of the Slave in
South Carolina, 1670-1740." *Journal of Southern
History*, 28 (November, 1962).

Spector, Robert M. "The Quock Walker Cases (1781-83)--
Slavery, Its Abolition, and Negro Citizenship in
Early Massachusetts." *Journal of Negro History*,
53 (January, 1968).

Starr, Raymond. "Historians and the Origins of British
North American Slavery." *Historian*, 36 (March,
1965).

Steel, Edward M., Jr. "Black Monongalians: A Judicial
View of Slavery and the Negro in Monongalia County,
1776-1865." *West Virginia History*, 34 (July,
1973).

Talmadge, John E. "Georgia Tests the Fugitive Slave
Law." *Georgia Historical Quarterly*, 49 (March,
1965).

Tyler, Ronnie C. "Fugitive Slaves in Mexico." *Journal
of Negro History*, 57 (January, 1972).

Wiecek, William M. "The Statutory Law of Slavery and
Race in the Thirteen Mainland Colonies of British
North America." *William and Mary Quarterly*, 34
(April, 1977).

Wilson, Benjamin C. "Kentucky Kidnappers, Fugitives,
and Abolitionists." *Michigan History*, 21 (1955).

Younger, Richard D. "Southern Grand Juries and Slavery." *Journal of Southern History*, 21 (April, 1955).

SLAVE DEMOGRAPHY

Bancroft, Frederic. *Slave-Trading in the Old South.* Baltimore: 1931.

Calderhead, William. "How Extensive Was the Border State Slave Trade? A New Look." *Civil War History*, 18 (March, 1972).

Clark, Thomas D. "The Slave Trade Between Kentucky and the Cotton Kingdom." *Mississippi Valley Historical Review*, 21 (December, 1934).

Cody, Cheryll Ann. "A Note on Changing Patterns of Slave Fertility in the South Carolina Rice District, 1735-1865." *Southern Studies*, 16 (Winter, 1977).

Cummings, John. *The Negro Population: 1790-1915.* Washington, D.C.: 1918.

Davis, Thomas J. "New York's Long Black Line: A Note on the Growing Slave Population, 1626-1790." *Afro-Americans in New York Life and History*, 2 (January, 1978).

Engerman, Stanley L. "Some Economic and Demographic Comparisons of Slavery in the United States and the British West Indies." *Economic History Review*, 29 (May, 1976).

Ernst, William J. "Changes in the Slave Population of the Virginia Tidewater and Piedmont, 1830-1860: A Stable Population Analysis." *Essays in History*, 19 (1975).

Godin, Claudia Dale. *Urban Slavery in the American South, 1820-1860: A Quantitative History.* Chicago: 1976.

Holland, C. G. "The Slave Population in the Plantation of John C. Cohoon, Jr., Nansemond County, Virginia, 1811-1863: Selected Demographic Characteristics." *Virginia Magazine of History and Biography*, 80 (July, 1972).

Hawkins, C. Homer. "Trends in Black Migration From 1863 to 1965." *Phylon*, 24 (June, 1973).

Klein, Herbert S. "Patterns of the Afro-American Population in the New World." In Nathan I. Huggins, et al. *Key Issues in the Afro-American Experience.* 1971

Klingman, D. Peter. "A Florida Slave Sale." *Florida Historical Quarterly*, 52 (July, 1973).

Kotlikoff, Lawrence J. and Sebastian E. Pinera. "The Old South's Stake in the Inter-Regional Movement of Slaves, 1850-1860." *Journal of Economic History*, 37 (June, 1977).

Kulikoff, Allan. "A 'Prolifick' People: Black Population Growth in the Chesapeake Colonies, 1700-1790." *Southern Studies*, 16 (Winter, 1977).

Laprade, William T. "The Domestic Slave Trade in the District of Columbia." *Journal of Negro History*, 11 (January, 1926).

Lowe, Richard B. and Randolph B. Campbell. "The Slave-Breeding Hypothesis: A Demographic Comment on the 'Buying' and 'Selling' States." *Journal of Southern History*, 42 (August, 1976).

Menard, Russell R. "The Maryland Slave Population, 1658 to 1730: A Demographic Profile of Blacks in Four Counties." *William and Mary Quarterly*, 32 (January, 1975).

Ricards, Sherman L. and George M. Blackburn. "A Demographic History of Slavery: Georgetown County, South Carolina, 1850." *South Carolina Historical Magazine*, 76 (October, 1975).

Rottenberg, Simon. "The Business of Slave Trading." *South Atlantic Quarterly*, 66 (Summer, 1967).

Smith, Julia F. "Slave Trading in Antebellum Florida." *Florida Historical Quarterly*, 50 (January, 1972).

Sweig, Donald M. "Reassessing the Human Dimension of the Interstate Slave Trade." *Prologue*, 12 (Spring, 1980).

Tadman, Michael. "Slave Trading in the Antebellum South: An Estimate of the Extent of the Inter-Regional Slave Trade." *Journal of American Studies*, 13 (August, 1979).

Taylor, A. A. "The Movement of Negroes from the East to the Gulf States from 1830 to 1850." *Journal of Negro History*, 8 (July, 1923).

Vinouskis, Maris A. "The Demography of the Slave Population in Antebellum America." *Journal of Interdisciplinary History*, 5 (Winter, 1975).

Wilkie, Jane Riblett. "The Black Urban Population of the Pre-Civil War South." *Phylon*, 37 (September, 1976).

Woodson, Carter G. *A Century of Negro Migration*. Washington, D.C.: 1918.

SLAVERY AND WAR

Abbott, Richard H. "Massachusetts and the Recruitment of Southern Negroes, 1863-1865." *Civil War History*, 4 (September, 1969).

Aptheker, Herbert. *The Negro in the American Revolution*. New York: 1940.

_____. *The Negro in the Civil War*. New York: 1938.

_____. "The Negro in the Union Navy." *Journal of Negro History*, 32 (April, 1947).

Berry, Mary F. "Negro Troops in Blue and Gray: The Louisiana National Guards, 1861-1863." *Louisiana History*, 8 (Spring, 1967).

Blassingame, John W. "The Recruitment of Negro Troops in Missouri during the Civil War." *Missouri Historical Review*, 58 (April, 1964).

Bond, Horace Mann. "The Negro in the Armed Forces of the United States Prior to World War I." *Journal of Negro Education*, 12 (Summer, 1943).

Bonsal Stephen. "The Negro Soldier in War and Peace." *North American Review*, 185 (June 7, 1907).

Brewer, James H. *The Confederate Negro: Virginia's Craftsmen and Military Laborers, 1861-1865*. Durham: 1969.

Brown, William Wells. *The Negro in the American Revolution*. Boston: 1855.

Cassell, Frank A. "Slaves of the Chesapeake Bay Area and the War of 1812." *Journal of Negro History*, 57 (April, 1972).

Cimprich, John. "Military Governor Johnson and Tennessee Blacks, 1862-1865." *Tennessee Historical Quarterly*, 39 (Winter, 1980).

Cornish, Dudley T. *The Sable Arm: Negro Troops in the Union Army, 1861-1865*. New York: 1956.

Coulter, C. Merton. "Slavery and Freedom in Athens, Georgia, 1860-1866." *Georgia Historical Quarterly*, 49 (September, 1965).

Crow, Jeffrey J. *The Black Experience in Revolutionary North Carolina*. Raleigh: 1977.

Curlee, Abigail. "The History of a Texas Slave Plantation, 1861-1863." *Southwestern Historical Quarterly*, 26 (Winter, 1922).

Dibble, Ernest F. "Slave Rentals to the Military: Pensacola and the Gulf Coast." *Civil War History*, 23 (June, 1977).

DuBois, W. E. B. *The Gift of Black Folk: The Negroes in the Making of America*. Boston: 1924.

Emilio, Luis A. *Brave Black Regiment: A History of the 54th Massachusetts*. Boston: 1891.

Escott, Paul D. "The Context of Freedom: Georgia's Slaves During the Civil War." *Georgia Historical Quarterly*, 58 (Spring, 1974).

Farley, M. Foster. "The South Carolina Negro During the American Revolution, 1775-1783." *Afro-American History*, 3 (December, 1972).

Foner, Jack D. *Blacks in the Military in American History: A New Perspective*. New York: 1974.

Gough, Robert J. "Black Men and the Early New Jersey Militia." *New Jersey History*, 88 (Winter, 1970).

Greene, Jack P. "'Slavery or Independence': Some Reflections on the Relationship among Liberty, Black Bondage, and Equality in Revolutionary South Carolina." *South Carolina Historical Magazine*, 80 (July, 1979).

Hartgrove, W. B. *The Negro Soldier in the American Revolution*. New York: 1915.

Hay, Thomas R. "The Question of Arming the Slaves." *Mississippi Valley Historical Review*, 6 (June, 1919).

Hughes, John Starrett. "Lafayette County and the Aftermath of Slavery, 1861-1870." *Missouri Historical Review*, 75 (October, 1980).

Jackson, Luther P. "Virginia Negro Soldiers and Seamen in the American Revolution." *Journal of Negro History*, 27 (July, 1942).

Kolchin, Peter. *First Freedom: The Responses of Alabama's Blacks to Emancipation and Reconstruction*. Westport: 1972.

Langley, Harold D. "The Negro in the Navy and Merchant Service--1789-1860." *Journal of Negro History*, 52 (October, 1967).

Litwack, Leon F. *Been in the Storm So Long: The Aftermath of Slavery*. New York: 1979.

95

Logan, Gwendolyn Evans. "The Slave in Connecticut During the American Revolution." *Connecticut Historical Society Bulletin*, (July, 1965).

Long, Howard H. "The Negro Soldier in the Army of the United States." *Journal of Negro Education*, 12 (Summer, 1973).

Longacre, Edward G. "Black Troops in the Army of the James." *Military Affairs*, 45 (February, 1981).

McConnell, Roland C. *Negro Troops of Antebellum Louisiana*. Baton Rouge: 1968.

MacLeod, Duncan J. *Slavery, Race, and the American Revolution*. London: 1974.

McPherson, James M. *The Negro's Civil War: How American Negroes Felt and Acted During the War for the Union*. New York: 1965.

Messner, William F. "Black Education in Louisiana, 1863-1865." *Civil War History*, 22 (March, 1976).

_____. *Freedmen and the Ideology of Free Labor: Louisiana, 1862-1865*. Lafayette: 1978.

Nell, William C. *The Colored Patriots of the American Revolution*. Boston: 1855.

_____. *Colored Americans in the Wars of 1776 and 1812*. Philadelphia: 1902.

Nelson, B. H. "Some Aspects of Negro Life in North Carolina During the Civil War." *North Carolina Historical Review*, 26 (April, 1949).

Quarles, Benjamin. "The Colonial Militia and Negro Manpower." *Mississippi Valley Historical Review*, 45 (March, 1959).

_____. *The Negro in the American Revolution*. Chapel Hill: 1940.

_____. *The Negro in the Civil War*. Boston: 1954.

Reid, Robert D. "The Negro in Alabama During the Civil War." *Journal of Negro History*, 35 (July, 1950).

Ripley, C. Peter. *Slaves and Freedmen in Civil War Louisiana*. Baton Rouge: 1977.

Smith, John David. "The Recruitment of Negro Soldiers in Kentucky, 1863-1865." *Register of the Kentucky Historical Society*, 72 (October, 1974).

Taylor, Joe Gray. "Slavery in Louisiana During the Civil War." *Louisiana History*, 8 (Winter, 1967).

Wesley, Charles H. "The Civil War and the Negro-American." *Journal of Negro History*, 47 (April, 1962).

_____. "The Employment of Negroes as Soldiers in the Confederate Army." *Journal of Negro History*, 4 (July, 1919).

Wiley, Bell Irvin. *Southern Negroes, 1861-1865.* New Haven: 1938.

Williams, George W. *A History of Negro Troops in the War of the Rebellion.* New York: 1888.

Williamson, Joel. *After Slavery: The Negro in South Carolina During Reconstruction, 1861-1877.* New York: 1975.

Wilson, Joseph T. *The Black Phalanx.* Hartford: 1888.

Wish, Harvey. "Slave Disloyalty under the Confederacy." *Journal of Negro History*, 23 (October, 1938).

Young, Tommy R. "The United States Army and the Institution of Slavery in Louisiana, 1803-1815." *Louisiana Studies*, 13 (Fall, 1974).

Chapter 6
The World of the Slaves

SLAVE SOCIETY

Applewaite, Joseph Davis. "Some Aspects of Society in Rural South Carolina in 1850." *North Carolina Historical Review*, 29 (January, 1952).

Atherton, Lewis, ed. "Life, Labor and Society in Boone County, Missouri, 1834-1852." *Missouri Historical Review*, 38 (April, 1944).

Berlin, Ira. "Time, Space, and the Evolution of Afro-American Society on British Mainland North America." *American Historical Review*, 85 (February, 1980).

Blanton, Wyndham B. *Medicine in Virginia in the Eighteenth Century*. Richmond: 1931.

Cohn, Raymond L. and Richard A. Jensen. "Mortality Rates and the Slave Trader." *Essays in Economic and Business History*, (1981).

Crum, Mason. *Gullah: Negro Life in the Carolina Sea Islands*. Durham: 1940.

De Grummond, Jewel Lynn. "Social History of St. Mary's Parish, 1845-1860." *Louisiana Historical Quarterly*, 32 (January, 1944).

Genovese, Eugene D. "Privileged Bondsmen and the Process of Accomodation." *Journal of Social History*, 5 (Fall, 1971).

Goodfriend, Joyce D. "Burghers and Blacks: The Evolution of a Slave Society at New Amsterdam." *New York History*, 59 (April, 1978).

Harper, C. W. "House Servants and Field Hands: Fragmentation in the Antebellum Slave Community." *North Carolina Historical Review*, 55 (January, 1978).

Horowitz, Donald L. "Color Differentiation in the American Systems of Slavery." *Journal of Interdisciplinary History*, 3 (Winter, 1973).

Hunter, Francis L. "Slave Society on the Southern Plantation." *Journal of Negro History*, 7 (January, 1922).

Johnson, Guion G. *A Social History of the Sea Islands*. Chapel Hill: 1930.

Johnson, James Hugo. "A New Interpretation of the Domestic Slave System." *Journal of Negro History*, 18 (January, 1933).

Kiple, Kenneth and Virginia Himmelsteib Kiple. *Another Dimension to the Black Diaspora: Diet, Disease, and Racism*. Cambridge: 1981.

_____. "The African Connection: Slavery, Disease, and Racism." *Phylon*, 41 (September, 1980).

Kulikoff, Allan. "Black Society and the Economics of Slavery." *Maryland Historical Magazine*, 70 (Summer, 1975).

_____. "The Origins of Afro-American Society in Tidewater Maryland and Virginia, 1700 to 1790." *William and Mary Quarterly*, 35 (April, 1978).

Lane, Ann J., ed. *The Debate Over Slavery: Stanley Elkins and His Critics*. Urbana: 1971.

Lee Anne S. and Everett S. Lee. "The Health of Slaves and the Health of Freedmen: A Savannah Study." *Phylon*, 38 (June, 1977).

Miller, Randall M. *The Afro-American Slaves: Community or Chaos?* Malabar: 1981.

Mintz, S. W. "Toward an Afro-American History." *Journal of World History*, 13 (Summer, 1971).

Mitchell, M. C. "Health and the Medical Profession in the Lower South." *Journal of Southern History*, 10 (November, 1944).

Olson, Edwin. "Social Aspects of the Slave in New York." *Journal of Negro History*, 26 (January, 1941).

Owsley, Frank L. *Plain Folk of the Old South*. Baton Rouge: 1949.

Postell, William Daniels. *The Health of Slaves on Southern Plantations*. Baton Rouge: 1951.

Puckrein, Gary. "Climate, Health, and Black Labor in the English Americas." *Journal of American Studies*, 13 (August, 1979).

Ransom, Roger L. "Was It Really All That Great To Be A Slave?" *Agricultural History*, 48 (October, 1974).

Rodney, Walter. "Upper Guinea and the Significance of the Origins of Africans Enslaved in the New World." *Journal of Negro History*, 54 (October, 1969).

Menard, Russell. "From Servants to Slaves: The Transformation of the Chesapeake Labor System." *Southern Studies*, 16 (Winter, 1977).

Savitt, Todd L. *Medicine and Slavery: The Diseases and Health Care of Blacks in Antebellum Virginia.* Urbana: 1978.

Shryrock, Richard H. "Medical Practice in the Old South." *South Atlantic Quarterly*, 29 (April, 1930).

Sikes, Lewright. "Medical Care for Slaves: A Preview of the Welfare State." *Georgia Historical Quarterly*, 52 (December, 1968).

Swados, Felice. "Negro Health on the Ante-Bellum Plantations." *Bulletin of the History of Medicine*, 10 (1941).

Sydnor, Charles S. "Life Span of Mississippi Slaves." *American Historical Review*, 35 (1930).

Taylor, R. H. "Feeding Slaves." *Journal of Negro History*, 9 (April, 1924).

Thorpe, Earl. "Chattel Slavery and Concentration Camps." *Negro History Bulletin*, 25 (May, 1962).

Whitten, David O. "Medical Care of Slaves: Louisiana Sugar Region and South Carolina Rice District." *Southern Studies*, 16 (Summer, 1977).

SLAVE CULTURE

Abraham, Roger D. *Deep Down in the Jungle.* Chicago: 1970.

_____. *Positively Black.* Englewood Cliffs: 1969.

Allen, W. F., et al. *Slave Songs of the United States.* New York: 1871.

Anderson, John Q. "The New Orleans Voodoo Ritual Dance and Its Twentieth Century Survivals." *Southern Folklore Quarterly*, (December, 1960).

Armstrong, Orlando Kay. *Old Massa's People: The Old Slaves Tell Their Story.* Indianapolis: 1931.

101

Bailey, Beryl Loftman. "Toward a New Perspective in Negro English Dialectology." *American Speech*, (October, 1965).

Berry, Mary F. and John W. Blassingame. "Africa, Slavery, and the Roots of Contemporary Black Culture." *Massachusetts Review*, 18 (Autumn, 1977).

Botkin, Benjamin A., ed. *Lay My Burden Down: A Folk History of Slavery*. Chicago: 1945.

Brewer, J. Mason, ed. *American Negro Folklore*. Chicago: 1968.

Brotz, Howard, ed. *Negro Social and Political Thought, 1850-1920*. New York: 1927.

Brown, Cecelia R. "The Afro-American Contribution to Dance in the United States, 1619-1965." *Negro Heritage*, 14 (1975).

Burlin, Natalie C. *Negro Folk Songs*. New York: 1917.

Christensen, A. H. M. *Afro-American Folklore*. Boston: 1892.

Courlander, Harold. *Negro Folk Music, USA*. New York: 1963.

Crum, Mason. *Gullah: Negro Life in the Carolina Sea Islands*. Durham: 1940.

Dayrell, Elphistone. *Folk Stories From Southern Nigeria, West Africa*. London: 1910.

Dickson, Bruce D., Jr. "The 'John and Old Master' Stories and the World of Slavery: A Study in Folktales and History." *Phylon*, 35 (December, 1974.

Dillard, J. L. *Black English: Its History and Usage in the United States*. New York: 1972.

_____. "On the Beginnings of Black English in the New World." *Orbis*, 21 (No. 2, 1972).

Dorson, Richard M. *American Negro Folktales*. New York: 1967.

_____. *Negro Folktales in Michigan*. Cambridge: 1956.

DuBois, W. E. B. *Black Folk Tales Then and Now*. New York: 1939.

_____. *The Souls of Black Folk*. New York: 1953.

Dundes, Alan, ed. *Mother Wit from the Laughing Barrell*. Englewood Cliffs: 1973.

Dwyer, David. *An Introduction to West African Pidgin English.* East Lansing: 1967.

Elkins, Stanley M. "Culture Contacts and Negro Slavery." *Proceedings of the American Philosophical Society,* (April, 1963).

Ennis, Merlin, ed. *Umbundu: Folk Tales From Angola.* Boston: 1962.

Fischer, Miles Mark, ed. *Negro Slave Songs in the United States.* Ithaca: 1953.

Fortier, Alcee. *Louisiana Folk Tales.* Boston: 1895.

Fry, Gladys-Marie. *Night Riders in Black Folk History.* Knoxville: 1975.

Garrett, Romeo B. "African Survivals in American Culture." *Journal of Negro History,* 51 (October, 1966.

Gerber, A. "Uncle Remus Traced to the Old World." *Journal of American Folklore,* 6 (October, 1893).

Georgia Writers Program. *Drums and Shadows: Survival Studies Among the Georgia Coastal Negroes.* Athens: 1940.

Harris, Joel Chandler. *Mingo and Other Sketches in Black and White.* Boston: 1884.

_____. *Nights With Uncle Remus.* Boston: 1883.

_____. *Uncle Remus: His Songs and Sayings.* Boston: 1892.

_____. *Uncle Remus and His Friends.* Boston: 1899.

Gonzales, Ambrose E. *With Aesop Along the Black Border.* Columbia: 1924.

Hancock, Gordon B. "Three Elements of African Culture." *Journal of Negro History,* 8 (July, 1923).

Herskovits, Melville J. *The American Negro: A Study in Racial Crossing.* New York: 1928.

_____. *The Myth of the Negro Past.* Chicago: 1941.

Jablow, Alta. *An Anthology of West African Folklore.* London: 1961.

Joyner, Charles W. *Folk Song in South Carolina.* Columbia: 1971.

Hughes, Langston and Arna Bontemps, eds. *The Book of Negro Folklore.* New York: 1958.

Johnson, Guy B. *Folk Culture on St. Helena Island, South Carolina.* Chapel Hill: 1930.

Johnson, James Weldon and Rosamond J. Johnson, eds.
     The Book of American Negro Spirituals. New York:
     1940.

Jones, Charles C., Jr. *Negro Myths of the Georgia
     Coast.* Boston: 1881.

Jones, Le Roi. *Blues People: Negro Music in White
     America.* New York: 1963.

Katz, Bernard, ed. *Social Implications of Early Negro
     Music in the United States.* New York: 1969.

Kochman, Thomas, ed. *Rappin' and Stylin' Out.* Urbana:
     1972.

Krehbiel, Henry Edward. *Afro-American Folk Songs: A
     Study in Racial and National Music.* New York:
     1914.

Levine, Lawrence W. *Black Culture and Black Conscious-
     ness: Afro-American Folk Thought from Slavery to
     Freedom.* New York: 1977.

Loggins, Vernon. *The Negro Author: His Development
     in America.* New York: 1931.

Lovell, John. *Black Song: The Forge and the Flame, The
     Story of How the Afro-American Spiritual Was
     Hammered Out.* New York: 1972.

Moore, Jamie Gilliard. "Africanisms Among Blacks of
     the Sea Islands." *Journal of Black Studies,* 10
     (June, 1980).

Odum, Howard W. and Guy B. Johnson. *Negro Workaday
     Songs.* Chapel Hill: 1926.

_____. *The Negro and His Songs: A Study of Typical
     Negro Songs in the South.* New York: 1968.

Parrish, Lydia. *Slave Songs of the Georgia Sea Islands.*
     New York: 1942.

Powdermaker, Hortense. *After Freedom: A Cultural Study
     of the Deep South.* New York: 1968.

Puckett, Newbell Niles. *Folk Beliefs of the Southern
     Negro.* Chapel Hill: 1926.

Read, Allen W. "Bilingualism in the Middle Colonies,
     1725-1775." *American Speech,* 12 (April,
     1937).

Roediger, David. "The Meaning of Africa for the Ameri-
     can Slave." *Journal of Ethnic Studies,* 4 (Fall,
     1976).

Saxon, Lyle, Edward Dreyer, and Robert Tallant.
     Gumbo Ya-Ya. New York: 1945.

Southern, Eileen. *The Music of Black Americans, A History*. New York: 1971.

Stewart, William A. "Sociolinguistic Factors in the History of American Negro Dialect." *Florida Foreign Languages Reporter*, 5 (Spring, 1966).

_____. "Continuity and Change in American Negro Dialects." *Florida Foreign Languages Reporter*, 6 (Spring, 1967).

Stuckey, Sterling. "Through the Prism of Folklore: The Black Ethos in Slavery." *Massachusetts Review*, 9 (1968).

Suttles, William C. "African Religious Survivals as Factors in American Slave Revolts." *Journal of Negro History*, 56 (April, 1971).

Szwed, John J. "Afro-American Musical Adaptation." *Journal of American Folklore*, 80 (March, 1969).

Tallant, Robert. *Voodoo in New Orleans*. New York: 1946.

Thorpe, Earl E. *The Mind of the Negro: An Intellectual History of Afro-Americans*. Baton Rouge: 1961.

Turner, Lorenzo D. *Africanisms in the Gullah Dialect*. Chicago: 1949.

_____. "African Survivals in the New World with Special Emphasis on the Arts." In *Africa Seen by American Negro Scholars*. New York: 1963.

Valenti, Suzanne. "The Black Diaspora: Negritude in the Poetry of West Africans and Black Americans." *Phylon*, 34 (December, 1973).

Vlach, John Michael. *The Afro American Tradition in Decorative Arts*. Cleveland: 1978.

Waterman, Richard A. "African Influence on the Music of the Americas." In Sol Tax, *Acculturation in the Americas*. Chicago: 1952.

Weisbord, Robert G. *Ebony Kinship: Africa, Africans, and the Afro-American*. Westport: 1973.

Whitten, Norman E. and John F. Szwed, eds. *Afro-American Anthropology: Contemporary Perspectives on Theory and Research*. New York: 1970.

Williamson, Juanita and Virginia Burke, eds. *A Various Language*. New York: 1971.

Work, John W. *American Negro Songs and Spirituals*. New York: 1940.

Works Progress Administration. *The Negro in Virginia.*
New York: 1940.

SLAVE RELIGION

Bailey, Kenneth K. "Protestantism and Afro-Americans
in the Old South: Another Look." *Journal of
Southern History*, 41 (November, 1975).

Bardley, Michael R. "The Role of the Black Church in
the Colonial Slave Society." *Louisiana Studies*,
14 (Winter, 1975).

Bennett, Robert A. "Black Episcopalians: A History
From the Colonial Period to the Present." *Historical Magazine of the Protestant Episcopal Church*,
43 (September, 1974).

Boham, Venita M. "Mysticism and the Afro-American Religious Experience." *Journal of Religious Thought*,
35 (Spring and Summer, 1978).

Bradley, L. Richard. "The Lutheran Church and Slavery."
Concordia Institute Historical Quarterly, 44
(February, 1971).

Brooks, Walter H. "The Evolution of the Negro Baptist
Church." *Journal of Negro History*, 7 (January, 1922).

Burton, William. *The Magic Drum.* New York: 1961.

Christiano, David. "Synod and Slavery, 1855." *New
Jersey History*, 40 (Spring, 1972).

Clarke, T. Erskine. "An Experiment in Paternalism:
Presbyterians and Slaves in Charleston, South
Carolina." *Journal of Presbyterian History*, 53
(Fall, 1975).

_____. *Wrestlin' Jacob: A Portrait of Religion in
the Old South.* Atlanta: 1979.

Clifton, Denzil T. "Anglicanism and Negro Slavery in
Colonial America." *Historical Magazine of the
Protestant Episcopal Church*, 39 (March, 1970).

Daniel, W. Harrison. "Southern Presbyterians and the
Negro in the Early National Period." *Journal of
Negro History*, 58 (July, 1973).

_____. "Southern Protestantism and the Negro, 1860-
1865." *North Carolina Historical Review*, 41 (July,
1964).

_____. "Virginia Baptists and the Negro in the Early
Republic." *Virginia Magazine of History and Biography*, 80 (January, 1972).

_____ . "Virginia Baptists and the Negro in the Antebellum Era." *Journal of Negro History*, 56 (January, 1971).

Danquah, J. B. *The Akan Idea of God*. London: 1944.

DuBois, W. E. B. *The Souls of Black Folk*. New York: 1953.

Durden, Robert F. "The Establishment of Calvary Protestant Episcopal Church for Negroes in Charleston." *South Carolina Historical Magazine*, 45 (April, 1964).

Epstein, Dena J. *Sinful Times and Spirituals: Black Folk Music to the Civil War*. Urbana: 1977.

Essig, James David. "A Very Wintry Season: Virginia Baptists and Slavery, 1785-1797." *Virginia Magazine of History and Biography*, 88 (April, 1980).

Fish, John O. "Southern Methodism and Accomodation of the Negro, 1902-1915." *Journal of Negro History*, 55 (July, 1970).

Forde, C. Daryll, ed. *African Worlds: Studies in the Cosmological Ideas and Social Values of African Peoples*. London: 1954.

Fordham, Monroe. *Major Themes in Northern Black Religious Thought, 1800-1860*. Hicksville: 1975.

Frazier, E. Franklin. *The Negro Church in America*. New York: 1964.

Freeman, Edward A. "Negro Baptist History." *Baptist History and Heritage*, 4 (July, 1969).

Genovese, Eugene D. "Black Plantation Preachers in the Slave South." *Louisiana Studies*, 11 (Fall, 1972).

Gravely, William B. "Early Methodism and Slavery: The Roots of a Tradition." *Wesleyan Quarterly Review*, (May, 1965).

Greenberg, Michael. "Slavery and the Protestant Ethic." *Louisiana Studies*, 15 (Fall, 1976).

Hamilton, Charles V. *The Black Preacher in America*. New York: 1973.

Harrison, W. P. *The Gospel Among the Slaves*. Nashville: 1893.

Hartzell, J. C. "Methodism and the Negro in the United States." *Journal of Negro History*, 8 (July, 1923).

Haynes, Leonard L. *The Negro Community Within American Protestantism, 1619-1844*. Boston: 1954.

Idowa, E. Bolaji. *Olodumare: God in Yoruba Belief*. London: 1962.

Jackson, James Conroy. "The Religious Education of the Negro in South Carolina Prior to 1850." *Historical Magazine of the Protestant Episcopal Church*, 36 (March, 1967).

Jackson, Luther P. "Religious Development of the Negro In Virginia from 1760 to 1860." *Journal of Negro History*, 16 (April, 1931).

_____. "Religious Instruction of Negroes, 1830 to 1860, with Special Reference to South Carolina." *Journal of Negro History*, 15 (January, 1930).

Jentz, John. "A Note on Genovese's Account of the Slaves' Religion." *Civil War History*, 23 (June, 1977).

Jernegan, Marcus W. "Slavery and Conversion in the American Colonies." *American Historical Review*, 21 (April, 1916).

Johnson, Guion G. "The Camp Meeting in Ante-Bellum North Carolina." *North Carolina Historical Review*, 10 (April, 1933).

Johnson, James Weldon and Rosamond J. Johnson, eds. *The Book of American Negro Spirituals*. New York: 1940.

Johnston, Ruby F. *The Development of Negro Religion*. New York: 1954.

Jones, Charles C. *The Religious Instruction of the Negroes in the United States*. New York: 1842.

Jones, Jerome W. "The Established Virginia Church and the Conversion of Negroes and Indians, 1620-1760." *Journal of Negro History*, 46 (January, 1961).

Jones, Lawrence N. "Black Christians in Antebellum America: In Quest of the Beloved Community." *Journal of Religious Thought*, 38 (Spring-Summer, 1981).

Lawrence, James B. "Religious Education of the Negro in the Colony of Georgia." *Georgia Historical Quarterly*, 14 (March, 1930).

Long, Durward. "The Methodist Church and Negro Slavery in America, 1784-1844." *Wesleyan Quarterly Review*, (February, 1966).

Lovell, John. *Black Song: The Forge and the Flame. The Story of How the Afro-American Spiritual Was Hammered Out*. New York: 1972.

Mathews, Donald. *Slavery and Methodism: A Chapter in American Morality, 1780-1845.* Princeton: 1965.

Mays, Benjamin Elizah. *The Negro's God as Reflected in His Literature.* New York: 1969.

Mays, Benjamin E. and Joseph W. Nicholson. *The Negro's Church.* New York: 1933.

Mbiti, John S. *African Religion and Philosophy.* New York: 1969.

_____. *New Testament Eschatology in an African Background.* New York: 1971.

_____. *The Prayers of African Religion.* New York: 1975.

Miller, Randall M. "'It is good to be religious': A Loyal Slave on God, Masters, and the Civil War." *North Carolina Historical Review*, 54 (January, 1977).

Mitchell, Henry H. "Towards a Black Evangelism." *Journal of Religious Thought*, 35 (Spring-Summer, 1978).

Moore, LeRoy, Jr. "The Spiritual: Soul of Black Religion." *Church History*, 40 (March, 1971).

Murray, Andrew F. *Presbyterians and the Negro: A History.* Philadelphia: 1966.

O'Brien, John T. "Factory, Church, and Community: Blacks in Antebellum Richmond." *Journal of Southern History*, 44 (November, 1978).

Parrinder, Geoffrey. *African Mythology.* London: 1967.

_____. *African Traditional Religion.* London: 1962.

_____. *Witchcraft: European and African.* London: 1958.

Perkins, Haven P. "Religion for Slaves: Difficulties and Methods." *Church History*, 10 (September, 1941).

Phillips, C. H. *History of the Colored Methodist Episcopal Church in America.* Jackson: 1925.

Pilcher, George William. "Samuel Davies and the Instruction of Negroes in Virginia." *Virginia Magazine of History and Biography*, 74 (July, 1966).

Posey, Walter B. "Influence of Slavery Upon the Methodist Church in the Early South and Southwest." *Mississippi Valley Historical Review*, 17 (March, 1931).

_____. *The Baptist Church in the Lower Mississippi Valley, 1776-1845.* Lexington: 1957.

Raboteau, Albert J. "Slave Autonomy and Religion." *Journal of Religious Thought,* 38 (Winter, 1982).

_____. *Slave Religion: The "Invisible Institution" in the Antebellum South.* New York: 1978.

Reilly, Timothy F. "Slavery and the Southwestern Evangelist in New Orleans, 1800-1861." *Journal of Mississippi History,* 41 (November, 1979).

Roediger, David R. "And Die in Dixie: Funerals, Death, and Heaven in the Slave Community, 1700-1865." *Massachusetts Review,* 22 (Spring, 1981).

Rushing, Byron. "A Note on the Origin of the African Orthodox Church." *Journal of Negro History,* 57 (January, 1972).

Simpson, George Eaton. *Black Religions in the New World.* New York: 1978.

Scherer, Lester B. *Slavery and Churches in Early America, 1619-1819.* Grand Rapids: 1975.

Sernett, Milton C. *Black Religion and American Evangelicalism: White Protestants, Plantation Missions, and the Flowering of Negro Christianity, 1787-1865.* Metuchen: 1975.

Smith, Timothy L. "Slavery and Theology: The Emergence of Black Christian Consciousness in Nineteenth-Century America." *Church History,* 41 (December, 1972).

Sobel, Mechal. "'They Can Never Both Prosper Together': Black and White Baptists in Nashville, Tennessee." *Tennessee Historical Quarterly,* 38 (Fall, 1979).

_____. *Trabelin' On: The Slave Journey to an Afro-Baptist Faith.* Westport: 1979.

Southern, Eileen. "Musical Practices in Black Churches of New York and Philadelphia, ca. 1800-1844." *Afro-Americans in New York Life and History,* 4 (January, 1980).

Stange, Douglas C. "Our Duty to Preach the Gospel to Negroes: Southern Lutherans and American Slavery." *Concordia Historical Institute Quarterly,* 42 (November, 1969).

Suttles, William C., Jr. "African Religious Survivals as Factors in American Slave Revolts." *Journal of Negro History,* 56 (April, 1971).

Taylor, Orville W. "Baptists and Slavery in Arkansas: Relationships and Attitudes." *Arkansas Historical Quarterly*, 38 (Autumn, 1979).

Thompson, J. Earl, Jr. "Slavery and Presbyterianism in the Revolutionary Era." *Journal of Presbyterian History*, 54 (Spring, 1976).

Thurman, Howard. *Deep River. Reflections on the Religious Insight of Certain of the Negro Spirituals.* New York: 1955.

_____. *The Negro Spiritual Speaks of Life and Death.* New York: 1947.

Todd, Willie G. "North Carolina Baptists and Slavery." *North Carolina Historical Review*, 24 (April, 1947).

Trimingham, J. Spencer. *A History of Islam in West Africa.* London: 1970.

Tucker, David M. *Black Pastors and Leaders: Memphis, 1819-1972.* Memphis: 1975.

Wamble, Gaston Hugh. "Negroes and Missouri Protestants Before and After the Civil War." *Missouri Historical Review*, 61 (April, 1967).

Washington, Joseph. *Black Religion.* Boston: 1964.

Whatley, George C., III. "The Alabama Presbyterian and His Slave, 1830-1864." *Alabama Review*, (January, 1960).

Wilmore, Gayrand S. *Black Religion and Black Radicalism.* Garden City: 1972.

Wilson, G. R. "The Religion of the American Negro Slave: His Attitude Toward Life and Death." *Journal of Negro History*, 8 (January, 1923).

Woodson, Carter G. *History of the Negro Church.* Washington, D.C.: 1921.

Work, John W. *American Negro Songs and Spirituals.* New York: 1940.

THE SLAVE FAMILY

Bernard, Jessie. *Marriage and Family Among Negroes.* Englewood Cliffs: 1966.

Billingsley, Andrew. *Black Families in White America.* Englewood Cliffs: 1969.

Blassingame, John W. *Black New Orleans, 1860-1880.* Chicago: 1973.

Blackburn, George and Sherman L. Ricards. "The Mother-Headed Family among Free Negroes in Charleston, South Carolina, 1850-1860." *Phylon*, 42 (Spring, 1981).

Bronwer, Merle G. "Marriage and Family Life Among Blacks in Colonial Pennsylvania." *Pennsylvania Magazine of History and Biography*, 94 (July, 1975).

Brown, Steven E. "Sexuality and the Slave Community." *Phylon*, 42 (Spring, 1981).

Burnham, Dorothy. "The Life of the Afro-American Woman in Slavery." *International Journal of Women's Studies*, 1 (July/August, 1978).

Chafe, William H. "Sex and Race: The Analogy of Social Control." *Massachusetts Review*, 18 (Spring, 1977).

Cody, Cheryll Ann. "A Note on Changing Patterns of Slave Fertility in the South Carolina Rice District, 1735-1865." *Southern Studies*, 16 (Winter, 1977).

_____. "Naming, Kinship, and Estate Dispersal: Notes on Slave Family Life on a South Carolina Plantation, 1786-1833." *William and Mary Quarterly*, 39 (January, 1982).

"The Cook Family in History." *Negro History Bulletin*, 9 (June, 1946).

Daniel, Constance E. H. "Two North Carolina Families--The Harrises and the Richardsons." *Negro History Bulletin*, 13 (October, 1949).

Douglas, Fannie H. "The David T. Howard Family." *Negro History Bulletin*, 17 (December, 1953).

DuBois, W. E. B. *The Negro American Family*. Atlanta: 1909.

Everly, Elaine C. "Marriage Registers of Freedmen." *Prologue*, 5 (Fall, 1973).

"The Family of Porter William Phillips." *Negro History Bulletin*, 27 (January, 1964).

"The Forten Family." *Negro History Bulletin*, 10 (January, 1947).

Frazier, E. Franklin. "The Negro Slave Family." *Journal of Negro History*, 15 (April, 1930).

_____. *The Free Negro Family: A Study of Family Origins before the Civil War*. Nashville: 1932.

112

_____. *The Negro Family in the United States*. Chicago: 1939.

Gutman, Herbert G. *The Black Family in Slavery and Freedom, 1750-1925*. New York: 1976.

Harley, Sharon and Rosalyn Terborg-Penn, eds. *The Afro-American Woman: Struggles and Images*. Port Washington: 1978.

Harris, William G. "Research on the Black Family: Mainstream and Dissenting Perspectives." *Journal of Ethnic Studies*, 6 (Winter, 1979).

Hays, William and Charles H. Mendel. "Extended Kinship Relations in Black and White Families." *Journal of Marriage and Family*, 35 (February, 1973).

Jackson, Luther P. "The Daniel Family of Virginia." *Negro History Bulletin*, 11 (December, 1947).

Jester, Annie Lash. *Domestic Life in Virginia in the Seventeenth Century*. Williamsburg: 1957.

"The Johnson Family." *Negro History Bulletin*, 12 (November, 1948).

Johnson, Guion G. "Courtship and Marriage Customs in Antebellum North Carolina." *North Carolina Historical Review*, 8 (October, 1931).

Johnson, Michael P. "Smothered Slave Infants: Were Slave Mothers at Fault?" *Journal of Southern History*, 47 (November, 1981).

Klein, Herbert S. and Stanley L. Engerman. "Fertility Differentials between Slaves in the United States and the British West Indies: A Note on Lactation Practices and Their Possible Implications." *William and Mary Quarterly*, 35 (April, 1978).

Klotter, James C. "Slavery and Race: A Family Perspective." *Southern Studies*, 17 (Winter, 1978).

Labinjoh, Justin. "The Sexual Life of the Oppressed: An Examination of the Family Life of Ante-Bellum Slaves." *Phylon*, 35 (December, 1974).

"The Leary Family." *Negro History Bulletin*, 10 (November, 1947).

Lewis, Ronald L. "Slave Families at Early Chesapeake Ironworks." *Virginia Magazine of History and Biography*, 86 (April, 1978).

"The Loguen Family." *Negro History Bulletin*, 10 (May, 1947).

McGettigan, James William, Jr. "Boone County Slaves: Sales, Estate Decisions, and Families, 1820-1865." *Missouri Historical Review*, 72 (January and April, 1978).

Moynihan, Daniel P. *The Negro Family: The Case for National Action*. Washington, D.C.: 1965.

Owsley, Frank Lawrence. *Plain Folk of the Old South*. Chicago: 1949.

Parkhurst, Jessie. "The Role of the Black Mammy in the Plantation Household." *Journal of Negro History*, 23 (July, 1938).

Pollard, Leslie J. "Aging and Slavery: A Gerontological Approach." *Journal of Negro History*, 46 (Fall, 1981).

Puckett, Newbell Niles. "American Negro Names." *Journal of Negro History*, 23 (January, 1938).

Ripley, C. Peter. "The Black Family in Transition: Louisiana, 1860-1865." *Journal of Southern History*, 41 (August, 1975).

Russell-Wood, A. J. R. "The Black Family in the Americas." *Societas*, 8 (Winter, 1978).

Savitt, Todd L. "Smothering and Overlaying of Virginia Slave Children: A Suggested Explanation." *Bulletin of the History of Medicine*, 49 (Fall, 1975).

Schweninger, Loren. "A Slave Family in the Ante-Bellum South." *Journal of Negro History*, 60 (January, 1975).

Sheeler, J. Reuben. "The Nabrit Family." *Negro History Bulletin*, 20 (October, 1956).

Sides, Sudie Duncan. "Slave Weddings and Religion: Plantation Life in Southern States Before the American Civil War." *History Today*, 24 (February, 1974).

Smallwood, James. "Emancipation and the Black Family: A Case Study in Texas." *Social Science Quarterly*, 57 (March, 1977).

Staples, Robert, ed. *The Black Family: Essays and Studies*. Belmont: 1971.

"The Tanner Family." *Negro History Bulletin*, 10 (April, 1947).

Steckel, Richard H. "Slave Marriage and the Family." *Journal of Family History*, 5 (Winter, 1980).

Taylor, Orville W. "'Jumping the Brookstick': Slave Marriage and Morality in Arkansas." *Arkansas Historical Quarterly*, 17 (Autumn, 1958).

"The Black Family." *The Black Scholar*, 5 (June, 1974).

Vacheenas, Jean and Betty Volk. "Born in Bondage: History of a Slave Family." *Negro History Bulletin*, 36 (May, 1973).

Wetherell, Charles. "Slave Kinship: A Case Study of the South Carolina Good Hope Plantation, 1835-1856." *Journal of Family History*, 6 (Fall, 1981).

White, John. "Whatever Happened to the Slave Family in the Old south?" *Journal of American Studies*, 8 (December, 1974).

Willie, Charles V. "The Black Family in America." *Dissent*, (February, 1971).

Woods, Frances Jerome. *Marginality and Identity: A Colored Creole Family Through Ten Generations*. Baton Rouge: 1972.

Woodson, Carter G. "The Record of the Clements." *Negro History Bulletin*, 9 (June, 1946).

_____. "The Gibbs Family." *Negro History Bulletin*, 11 (October, 1947).

_____. "Robert Smalls and His Descendents." *Negro History Bulletin*, 11 (November, 1947).

_____. "The Wormley Family." *Negro History Bulletin*, 11 (January, 1948).

_____. "The Waring Family." *Negro History Bulletin*, 11 (February, 1948).

SLAVE RESISTANCE

Addington, Wendell G. "Slave Insurrections in Texas." *Journal of Negro History*, 35 (October, 1950).

Aptheker, Herbert. *American Negro Slave Revolts*. New York: 1943.

_____. *Nat Turner's Slave Rebellion*. New York: 1966.

Bauer, Raymond A. and Alice H. Bauer. "Day to Day Resistance to Slavery." *Journal of Negro History*, 27 (October, 1942).

Berry, Mary Frances. *Black Resistance/White Law: A History of Constitutional Racism in America*. New York: 1971.

Bridner, Elwood L., Jr. "The Fugitive Slaves of Maryland." *Maryland Historical Magazine*, 66 (Spring, 1971).

Carroll, Joseph C. *Slave Insurrections in the United States, 1800-1865*. Boston: 1938.

Clark, John Hendrik, ed. *William Styron's Nat Turner: Ten Black Writers Respond*. Boston: 1968.

Cromwell, John W. "The Aftermath of Nat Turner's Insurrection." *Journal of Negro History*, 5 (January, 1920).

Crow, Jeffrey J. "Slave Rebelliousness and Social Conflict in North Carolina, 1775 to 1802." *William and Mary Quarterly*, 37 (January, 1980).

Davis, Thomas J. "The New York Slave Conspiracy of 1741 as Black Protest." *Journal of Negro History*, 56 (January, 1971).

Dew, Charles B. "Black Ironworkers and the Slave Insurrection Panic of 1856." *Journal of Southern History*, 41 (August, 1975).

Duff, John B. and Peter M. Mitchell, eds. *The Nat Turner Rebellion: The Historical Event and the Modern Controversy*. New York: 1971.

Farley, M. Foster. "A History of Negro Slave Revolts in South Carolina." *Afro-American Studies*, 3 (June, 1972).

_____. "The Fear of Negro Slave Revolts in South Carolina, 1690-1865." *Afro-American Studies*, 3 (December, 1972).

Fleming, John E. "The Stono River Rebellion and Its Impact on the South Carolina Slave Code." *Negro History Bulletin*, 42 (July-August, September, 1979).

Franklin, John Hope. "Slavery and the Martial South." *Journal of Negro History*, 38 (January, 1953).

Franklin, Vincent. "Slavery, Personality, and Black Culture--Some Theoretical Issues." *Phylon*, 35 (March, 1974).

Frederickson, George M. and Christopher Lasch. "Resistance to Slavery." *Civil War History*, 13 (December, 1967).

Genovese, Eugene D. *From Rebellion to Revolution: Afro American Slave Revolts in the Making of the Modern World*. Baton Rouge: 1979.

_____. "Rebelliousness and Docility in the Negro Slave: A Critique of the Elkins' Thesis." *Civil War History*, 13 (December, 1967).

_____. "When Slaves Left Old Marster." *Civil Liberties Review*, 2 (Winter, 1975).

Gordon, A. H. "The Struggle of the Slave for Physical Freedom." *Journal of Negro History*, 13 (January, 1928).

Granada, Ray. "Slave Unrest in Florida." *Florida Historical Quarterly*, 55 (July, 1976).

Greene, Lorenzo J. "Mutiny on the Slave Ships." *Phylon*, 5 (December, 1944).

Gross, Seymour L. and Eileen Bender. "History, Politics, and Literature: The Myth of Nat Turner." *American Quarterly*, 23 (October, 1971).

Halasz, Nicholas. *Rattling Chains: Slave Unrest and Revolt in the Antebellum South*. New York: 1966.

Harrington, Fred Harvey. "The Fort Jackson Mutiny." *Journal of Negro History*, 27 (October, 1942).

Higginson, Thomas Wentworth. *Black Rebellion*. New York: 1969.

Johnson, Michael P. "Runaway Slaves and the Slave Communities in South Carolina, 1799 to 1830." *William and Mary Quarterly*, 38 (July, 1981).

Jones, Howard. "The Peculiar Institution and National Honor: The Case of the *Creole* Slave Revolt." *Civil War History*, 21 (March, 1975).

Kilson, Marion. "Towards Freedom: An Analysis of Slave Revolts in the United States." *Phylon*, 25 (Summer, 1964).

Kneebone, John T. "Sambo and the Slave Narratives: A Note on Sources." *Essays in History*, 19 (1975).

Lannitz-Schurer, Leopold S., Jr. "Slave Resistance in Colonial New York: An Interpretation of Daniel Horsemanden's New York Conspiracy." *Phylon*, 41 (June, 1980).

Lloyd, Willis D. "The American Colonization Society and the Slave Recaptives of 1860-1861: An Early Example of United States--African Relations." *Journal of Negro History*, 47 (April, 1962).

Lofton, John M., Jr. "Denmark Vesey's Call to Arms." *Journal of Negro History*, 33 (October, 1948).

_____. *Insurrection in South Carolina: The Turbulent World of Denmark Vesey*. Yellow Springs: 1964.

Marszalek, John F. "Battle for Freedom--Gabriel's Insurrection." *Negro History Bulletin*, 39 (March, 1976).

McKenzie, Robert H. "The Shelby Iron Company: A Note on Slave Personality After the Civil War." *Journal of Negro History*, 58 (July, 1973).

McKibben, Davidson B. "Negro Slave Insurrections in Mississippi, 1800-1865." *Journal of Negro History*, 34 (January, 1949).

Meaders, Daniel E. "South Carolina Fugitives as Viewed Through Local Colonial Newspapers With Emphasis on Runaway Notices, 1732-1865." *Journal of Negro History*, 60 (April, 1975).

Messner, William F. "Black Violence and White Response: Louisiana, 1862." *Journal of Southern History*, 41 (February, 1975).

Milligan, John D. "Slave Rebelliousness and the Florida Maroon." *Prologue*, 6 (Spring, 1974).

Mullin, Gerald W. *Flight & Rebellion: Slave Resistance in Eighteenth-Century Virginia*. New York: 1972.

Mutunhu, Tendai. "Tompkins County: An Underground Railroad Transit in Central New York." *Afro-Americans in New York Life and History*, 3 (July, 1979).

Nadelhaft, Jerome. "The Somersett Case and Slavery: Myth, Reality, and Repercussions." *Journal of Negro History*, 51 (July, 1966).

Noonan, John T. *The Antelope: The Ordeal of the Recaptured Africans in the Administrations of James Monroe and John Quincy Adams*. Berkeley: 1977.

Phillips, Ulrich B. "Slave Crime in Virginia." *American Historical Review*, 20 (January, 1915).

Rachleff, Marshall. "Big Joe, Little Joe, Bill, and Jack: An Example of Slave Resistance in Alabama." *Alabama Review*, 32 (April, 1979).

Russell, Marion J. "American Slave Discontent in Records of the High Court." *Journal of Negro History*, 31 (October, 1946).

Schafer, Judith Kelleher. "The Immediate Impact of Nat Turner's Insurrection." *Louisiana History* (Fall, 1960).

Skemer, Don C. "New Evidence on Black Unrest in Colonial Brooklyn." *Long Island History*, 12 (Fall, 1975).

Stampp, Kenneth M. "Rebels and Sambos: The Search for the Negro's Personality in Slavery." *Journal of Southern History*, 37 (August, 1971).

Strother, Horatio T. *The Underground Railroad in Connecticut*. Middletown: 1962.

Suttles, William C., Jr. "African Religious Survivals as Factors in American Slave Revolts." *Journal of Negro History*, 56 (April, 1971).

Szasz, Ferenc M. "The New York Slave Revolt of 1741: A Re-Examination." *New York History*, 48 (July, 1967).

Towner, Lawrence W. "'A Fondness for Freedom': Servant Protest in Puritan Society." *William and Mary Quarterly*, 19 (July, 1962).

Tragle, Henry Irving. *The Southampton Slave Revolt of 1831*. Amherst: 1971.

Wade, Richard C. "The Vesey Plot: A Reconsideration." *Journal of Southern History*, 30 (May, 1964).

White William W. "The Texas Slave Insurrection of 1860." *Southwestern Historical Quarterly*, 53 (January, 1949).

Wish, Harvey. "American Slave Insurrections before 1861." *Journal of Negro History*, 22 (July, 1937).

Yanuck, Julius. "The Garner Fugitive Slave Case." *Mississippi Valley Historical Review*, 40 (June, 1953).

2A ½